MW01620296

HAIGA

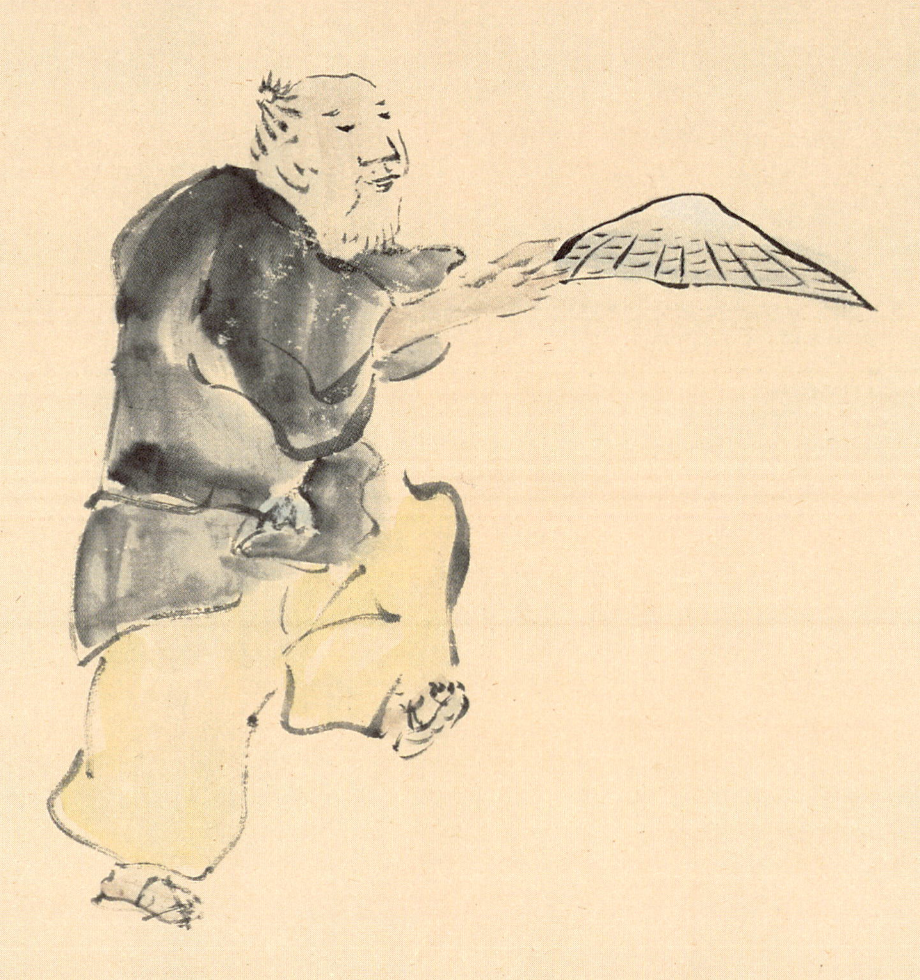

HAIGA

Takebe Sōchō and the Haiku-Painting Tradition

Let the light snow fall
I'll dance with my sedge hat
in front of the god

— *Takebe Sōchō*

Stephen Addiss

with an essay by Fumiko Y. Yamamoto

Marsh Art Gallery, University of Richmond
in association with
University of Hawai'i Press
Honolulu

Published on the occasion of the exhibition
Haiga: Takebe Sōchō and the Haiku-Painting Tradition

Marsh Art Gallery, University of Richmond, Virginia
March 3 through April 16, 1995

Spencer Museum of Art, The University of Kansas, Lawrence
August 27 through October 14, 1995

University Art Museum, University of California, Santa Barbara
November 8 through December 17, 1995

New Orleans Museum of Art, Louisiana
January 6 through March 3, 1996

Smith College Museum of Art, Northampton, Massachusetts
March 28 through May 26, 1996

The exhibition and publication are made possible with the generous support of an anonymous donor, Dr. Willie M. Reams, Jr., and the University of Richmond Cultural Affairs Committee.

This book and exhibition are dedicated to Masuda Shōzaburō.

Copublished by
Marsh Art Gallery,
University of Richmond,
in association with
University of Hawai'i Press,
2840 Kolowalu Street,
Honolulu, Hawai'i 96822

Production and printing
by The Arts Publisher, Richmond, Virginia
Printed in the United States of America

Library of Congress
Catalog Card Number 95-2329
ISBN 0-8248-1749-4 (cloth)
ISBN 0-8248-1750-8 (paper)

Cover:
Takebe Sōchō (1761-1814)
Discussions under a Mosquito Net
Ink and color on paper, 13 3/8 x 21 3/8 inches
Masuda Shōzaburō Collection, Tokyo
Cat. No. 26

Frontispiece:
Takebe Sōchō (1761-1814)
Screens of the Twelve Months (detail)
Ink and color on paper; two six-panel screens,
each 62 5/8 x 136 inches
Masuda Shōzaburō Collection, Tokyo
Cat. No. 18

Photograph Credits:

Owen F. Murphy, Jr., New Orleans: p. 61
New Orleans Museum of Art: pp. 113, 115, 121
Spencer Museum of Art, University of Kansas: p. 79
Trahan-Brocato Photo, courtesy of New Orleans Museum of Art: pp. 107, 111
Susumu Wakisaka, courtesy of Idemitsu Museum of Arts, Tokyo: pp. 27, 31
Katherine Wetzel, Richmond: cover, frontispiece, pp. 6, 13, 19, 64, 65, 66, 67, 71, 81, 85, 87, 93, 95, 108, 109

CONTENTS

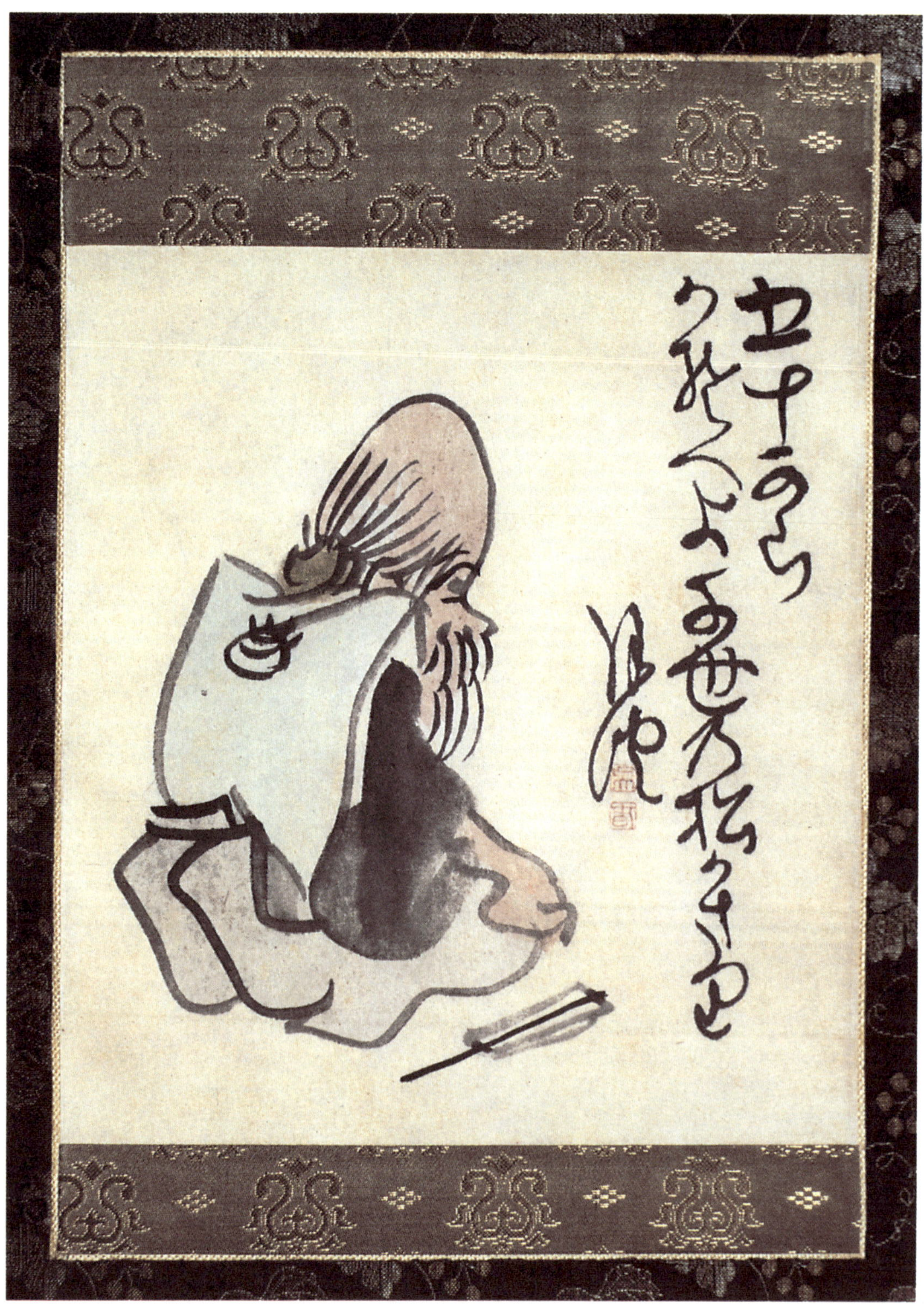

Matsumura Goshun (1752-1811), *Age Fifty*
Ink and light color on paper, 7 x 6 1/2 inches
Private Collection, Cat. No. 13

FOREWORD

This exhibition of haiga is part of the Marsh Art Gallery's programming focusing on aspects of Japanese art, which has become an essential part of our exhibition policy in recent years. To Stephen Addiss, our colleague as well as guest curator and author, we are indebted for this focus and especially for this exhibition and catalogue. To unexcelled knowledge of the field he adds both enthusiasm and a refreshing originality of thought. Since joining the faculty at the University of Richmond as Tucker-Boatwright Professor in the Humanities and Professor of Art History, he has not only enriched the course offerings in the study of art and art history but has deeply enriched the entire university community with his intellectual curiosity and energetic pursuance of scholarship. We join together in expressing thanks to Masuda Shōzaburō and the other lenders who have enabled us to realize the first exhibition in the United States devoted to haiga.

At the University of Richmond, our special appreciation goes to Dr. Richard L. Morrill, President; Dr. Zeddie P. Bowen, Vice President and Provost; and Dr. David E. Leary, Dean of the School of Arts and Sciences; for their continuing encouragement of the visual arts at the university through their support of important projects such as this exhibition being organized by its gallery. Special thanks go to Lynda Brown for her endless help and patience throughout the project, and to Chris Muzik and our student workers for their assistance during this exhibition. Finally, we acknowledge a debt of gratitude to Margaret Fields Denton, Charles Johnson, Mark Rhodes, and Ephraim Rubenstein, all colleagues in the Department of Art, for their contribution and support.

We would also like to thank William Hamilton and the University of Hawai'i Press for copublishing this catalogue. Our thanks go to James Witt and The Arts Publisher for so graciously handling the myriad details of the production of this book.

The exhibition and publication are made possible with the generous support of an anonymous donor, Dr. Willie M. Reams, Jr., and the University's Cultural Affairs Committee.

Richard Waller
Director, Marsh Art Gallery, University of Richmond

ACKNOWLEDGMENTS

My deepest thanks go first of all to Masuda Shōzaburō, to whom this book and exhibition are gratefully dedicated. I would also like to express my great appreciation to Fumiko Y. Yamamoto for her essay and for her advice on many aspects of the text, and to Teruko Segawa of the Kakimori Bunko for her help in reading difficult inscriptions. In addition, Kinuko Jambor was extremely gracious in assisting on haiku interpretations.

I would also like to thank Setsuko Beppu, Jonathan Chaves, Bruce Darling, Thomas Hare, Janet Ikeda, Masato Ozaki, Audrey Yoshiko Seo, Joseph Seubert, and Akira Yamamoto for their kind assistance and very useful suggestions, and to Rosalie West for her thoughtful editing. My special appreciation goes to Richard Waller, Director of the Marsh Art Gallery, who has been wonderfully supportive and enthusiastic throughout the lengthy preparation of this exhibition and catalogue. Finally, I am grateful to all the lenders of the fine haiga included here.

Stephen Addiss

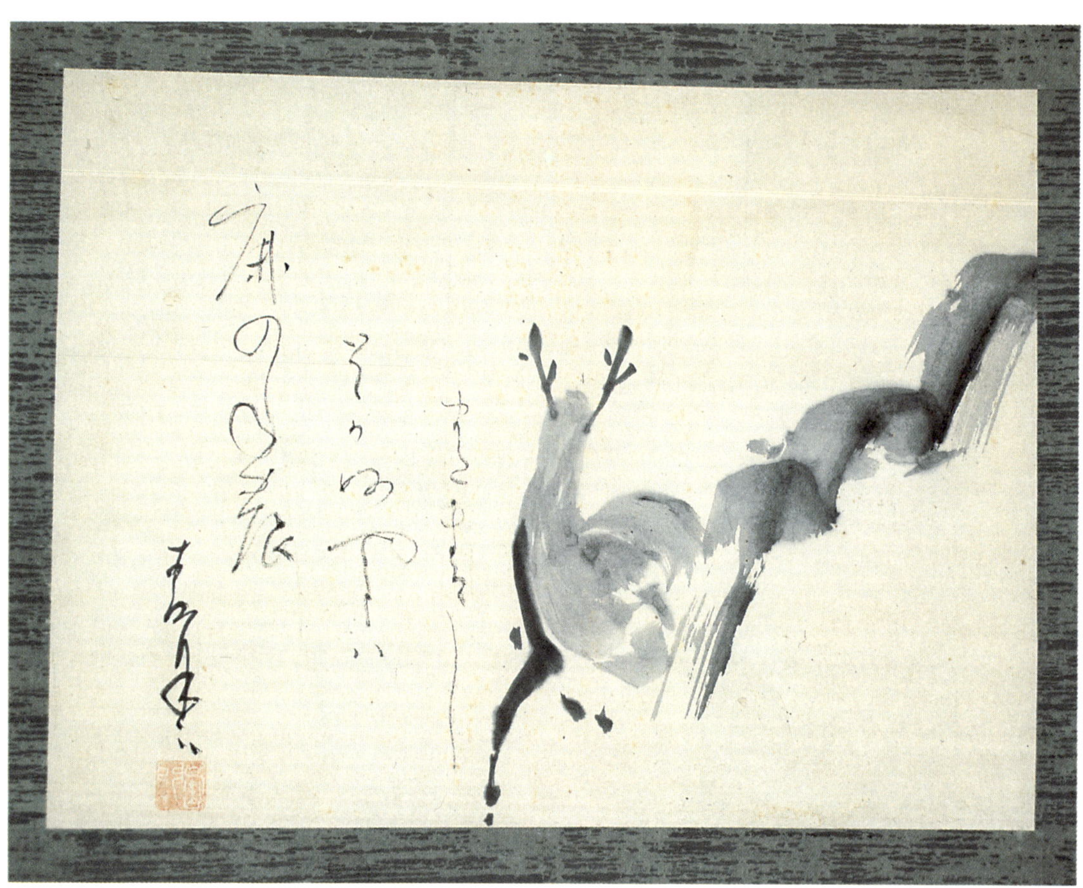

Nakagawa Otsuyu,
also known as Bakurin (1675-1739)
Deer
Ink on paper, 10 7/8 x 14 3/4 inches
Beckett Collection
Cat. No. 6

INTRODUCTION: HAIKU AND HAIGA

HAIGA is the special word for a unique form of art. HAI comes from haiku, previously known in Japan as *haikai* or *hokku,* three-line poems of 5, 7, 5 syllables; the word originally had the connotation of leisure or amusement. GA is the word for painting, so HAIGA means haiku-painting.

Haiku are familiar in the West, having been composed in English by famous poets as well as schoolchildren, but haiga are almost unknown. This book, accompanying the first exhibition of haiga in the United States, is intended to open the doors to a unique artform in which poetry, calligraphy, and painting add to each other's creative expression. We do not concentrate here upon works by the most skilled painters among haiku poets such as Yosa Buson (1716-1784), although his haiga are exceptional works of pure visual art (see Cat. Nos. 11, 12). Instead, we present the direct visual expression of Japanese poets who added further meanings to their words through images that are usually extremely modest. As the poet-artist Watanabe Kazan (1793-1841) once wrote:

Asagao wa heta no kaku sae aware nari	Morning glories — even clumsy drawings are full of emotion

In several haiga included here, such as the *Moon* by Inoue Shirō (1742-1812), the painting consists only of a single line (Cat. No. 37), and yet how expressive this one stroke of the brush can be! The Japanese aesthetic of the greatest effect from the least of means is especially true for haiga.

The major masters Bashō, Buson, and Issa are represented here, but as a way to explore haiga more deeply, we also present a number of works by Takebe Sōchō (1761-1814). This opportunity came from the kindness of Mr. Masuda Shōzaburō, who has the most extensive collection of works by Sōchō in Japan, and it offers us the chance to experience the full range of one representative poet-painter's work (Cat. Nos. 18-33). For comparison purposes, we include not only Sōchō's haiga, but also one painting with a *kyōka* (satiric five-line poem), one with a *kanshi* (Chinese-style poem), and one painting without any inscription, as well as two woodblock book illustrations. But it is his haiga that best represent Sōchō's poetic vision; seemingly the most relaxed and casual of his works, they focus upon the interstice where poem and image most fully join together.

It may seem odd to admire and study paintings that were not created primarily by painters, because in our own society we have honored the work of the finest professional artists almost to the exclusion of any others. In Japan, this has not been so, in part because of the close union of poetry, calligraphy, and painting. All three are created with the same tools of brush, paper, and ink by artists to whom poetic vision was paramount. The integration of the arts has been taken much further in Asia than in the West, and in Japan the depth of artistic spirit is considered more important than matters of training or technique. Since many poet-artists do not have to earn their living by selling their works, they can express moments of heightened awareness freely and directly. Haiga combines words and images without any need for commercial appeal.

In a fine haiga, the poem does not just explain the painting, nor does the painting merely illustrate the poem. Instead, they add layers of meaning to each other. This form of aesthetics derives from the nature of haiku itself as a poetic medium developed in Japan over the past five hundred years. An abbreviated form of poetry that evokes more than it directly states, haiku opens the door to the reader's own perception. Similarly, haiku-painting does not present elaborate images, but rather suggests shapes and forms to be completed in the viewer's imagination. Both haiku and haiga are arts of process rather than product; this process becomes complete when we are stimulated to draw upon our own imagination to fulfill the meanings of the poem and image.

The three-line haiku emerged from Japanese poetic tradition in the sixteenth century. Previously, the most celebrated Japanese verses had been *waka* (also called *tanka),* five-line poems composed of 5, 7, 5, 7, 7 syllables and considered, like all Japanese poetry, as a form of song *(uta). Waka* reached their peak in the Heian and Kamakura periods (794-1336), as mastered by the aristocratic class of emperors, courtiers, and court ladies, although they were also composed by Buddhist monks.

Over time, poets enjoyed composing poems together, creating the longer *renga* form from the *waka* tradition. One poet would begin with three lines of 5, 7, 5 syllables, another would add two lines of 7 syllables each, still another would contribute three lines of 5, 7, 5, and so on. The importance of such interactive poetry grew until *renga* became the most significant poetic form of the fifteenth and sixteenth centuries. It was not necessary to carry on the specific thought or image of the previous lines to create fine *renga.* Instead, moving the poem subtly in a new direction was highly honored. In effect, each addition contributed another layer of meaning to the total *renga,* which might continue for hundreds of lines.

Eventually, the individual segments of *renga* began to be enjoyed as small poetic formats in themselves. Because of the Japanese taste for asymmetry, the three lines of 5, 7, 5 syllables became more popular than 7, 7 syllable couplets, and haiku was born. The crucial realization was that the seeming "incompleteness" of a single section of *renga* could become a virtue, allowing listeners and readers to complete the poem in their own minds.

Comparing the earlier form of *waka* to haiku shows a major change of poetic values. Typical courtly *waka* utilize nature imagery to express personal emotion, often the joys and pangs of love. One example by Tsumori Kunimoto (1023-1103) compares nature to the art of calligraphy:

Usuzumi ni kaku tamazusa to miyurukana kasumeru sora ni kaeru karigane	Like a love letter written in subtle shades of ink — in the hazy sky, returning wild geese

Haiku tend to be less romantic, often combining a touch of humor with down-to-earth perceptions. A haiku by Kobayashi Issa (1763-1827) suggests a different image of wild geese:

Kari waya waya ore ga uwasa o itasu kana	Wild geese murmuring — are they spreading gossip about me?

This lack of pretention comes from the nature of haiku as poetry, which is to pay close attention to everyday things and find them extraordinary. Where court poets had celebrated the perfect autumn moon, Matsuo Bashō (1644-1694) wrote:

kumo ori ori hito wo yasumeru tsukimi kana	From time to time clouds give us rest from viewing the moon

Another verse by Bashō changes the focus of attention during moon-viewing:

Tsukimi suru
za ni utsukushiki
kao mo nashi

Among those
moon-viewing, not one
beautiful face

This haiku could be understood as criticizing people who seek outside themselves for what they need, as mocking the hypocrisy of those who pretend to see beauty but do not reflect it in themselves, or simply as an observation of humanity when it does not observe itself.

Understanding the change from *waka* to haiku poetry helps to make clear the corresponding evolution from the earlier court-influenced poem-paintings to haiga, from refined and detailed styles to free and simple brushwork. This change began with the birth of haiku; just as elegant and romantic *waka* were not always comfortable formats in which later poets could express their down-to-earth poetic perceptions, detailed and colorful paintings could not fully suggest the visual significance of the everyday world. One important factor in the change was the entry of many more people into the ranks of poets and artists. Previously, verse had generally been confined to highly educated courtiers and monks, and painting had usually been restricted to those with elaborate formal training and official patronage. Yet every literate person was familiar with brush, ink, and paper, the basic materials of poetry, calligraphy and painting. It is no coincidence, therefore, that the development of haiku and haiga took place as education and cultural experience became available to a much wider populace, especially during the peaceful and prosperous centuries after the unification of Japan under Tokugawa rule in 1600.

However, another important factor in the aesthetics of haiku and haiga was the influence of Zen. Although this form of Buddhism had been an important cultural influence in Japan from the time of its introduction in the thirteenth century, it only gradually began to permeate the poetic consciousness of everyday people. During the centuries when Japan was ruled by a warrior culture, Zen had been primarily the religion of rulers and samurai, but in the seventeenth century the Tokugawa government turned its support to Neo-Confucianism. As a result, major Zen Masters such as Hakuin Ekaku (1685-1768) reached out to farmers, craftsmen, housewives, and townspeople more than had most of his predecessors. As part of this process, Hakuin and his followers created some haiga of their own (see Cat. Nos. 45-47). Furthermore, Bashō himself studied Zen; the American Zen Master Robert Aitken has written a fascinating book called *A Zen Wave* that studies Bashō's haiku as progressive stages in the poet's Zen consciousness.

Buson also wrote about haiku and Zen, stating in his *Preface to the Haiku of Shundai* that the essence of haiku was to use ordinary language to go beyond the ordinary. He once referred to Hakuin's famous *kōan* (meditation question), "What is the sound of one hand clapping?" as the Zen of haiku poetry. In both, the focus upon everyday life becomes a means of transcendence. There is no need for romantic ideals or refined images; like Zen, haiku and haiga ask that we pay attention to what is right here, right now.

Or else it's gone. As Bashō's fish-merchant pupil Sampū (1647-1732) wrote:

Yuku uma no
ato sae atsuki
hokori kana

The horse passes —
nothing left but
hot dust

Despite their similarities, however, there are several differences between haiga and Zen. For example, most Zen paintings (known as *Zenga)* have inscriptions in Chinese. When they qualify as haiga by including a haiku poem, their primary function is still Zen teaching. Therefore they often have extremely bold images rather than lyrical evocations of human responses to nature. For this reason the haiga of Zen Masters is much less likely than other haiga to contain a seasonal reference, such as the cherry blossoms of spring, or the full moon of autumn.

Four poems by Bashō demonstrate the importance of the seasons in the world of poetry; the first three convey redolent images of summer through the senses of sight, smell, and hearing:

Samidare ni tsuru no ashi mijikaku nari	Rainy season — the crane's legs grow shorter
Namagusashi konagi ga ue no hae no wata	From the weeds — the smell of fish guts
Ushibeya ni ka no koe kuraki zansho kana	In the cowshed mosquito voices darken — late summer heat

In contrast, a fourth haiku by Bashō captures the chill of winter through imaginative empathy:

Kogarashi ni iwa fuki togaru sugima kana	Winter wind through the cedars sharpens the rocks

This kind of clear perception has been a hallmark of the finest haiku since its inception. Once it evolved out of *renga,* the history of haiku can be summed up very simply. Although at times some Japanese haiku poets favored cleverness, wit, and wordplay, the major masters such as Bashō, Buson, and Issa insisted on returning to direct human experience. The point of haiku is to perceive, understand and express the beauty of the seemingly commonplace, as in Bashō's verse:

Chō no tobu bakari nonaka no hikage kana	Only butterflies — flitting in the sunshadow of the fields

To turn this haiku into a haiga, what kind of image would be appropriate? It would not be necessary to depict exactly what is described in the words. Instead, some aspect of the haiku might be painted with a few swift lines, such as a butterfly, or grasses of the fields, or even just the play of sun and shadow. The painting might even have a completely different subject than the poem; as long as it suggested the evanescent movement of light and darkness, it would become a complementary visual haiku, focusing attention on an everyday scene, and offering each viewer the opportunity to complete the work in his or her own mind's eye.

Haiga is more than the sum of its parts — poem, painting, the combination of the two, and whatever further experiences, memories, and images that these may suggest to each viewer. This multiplicity arising from apparent simplicity is the outstanding characteristic of haiga, making it a unique genre within the world of Japanese art.

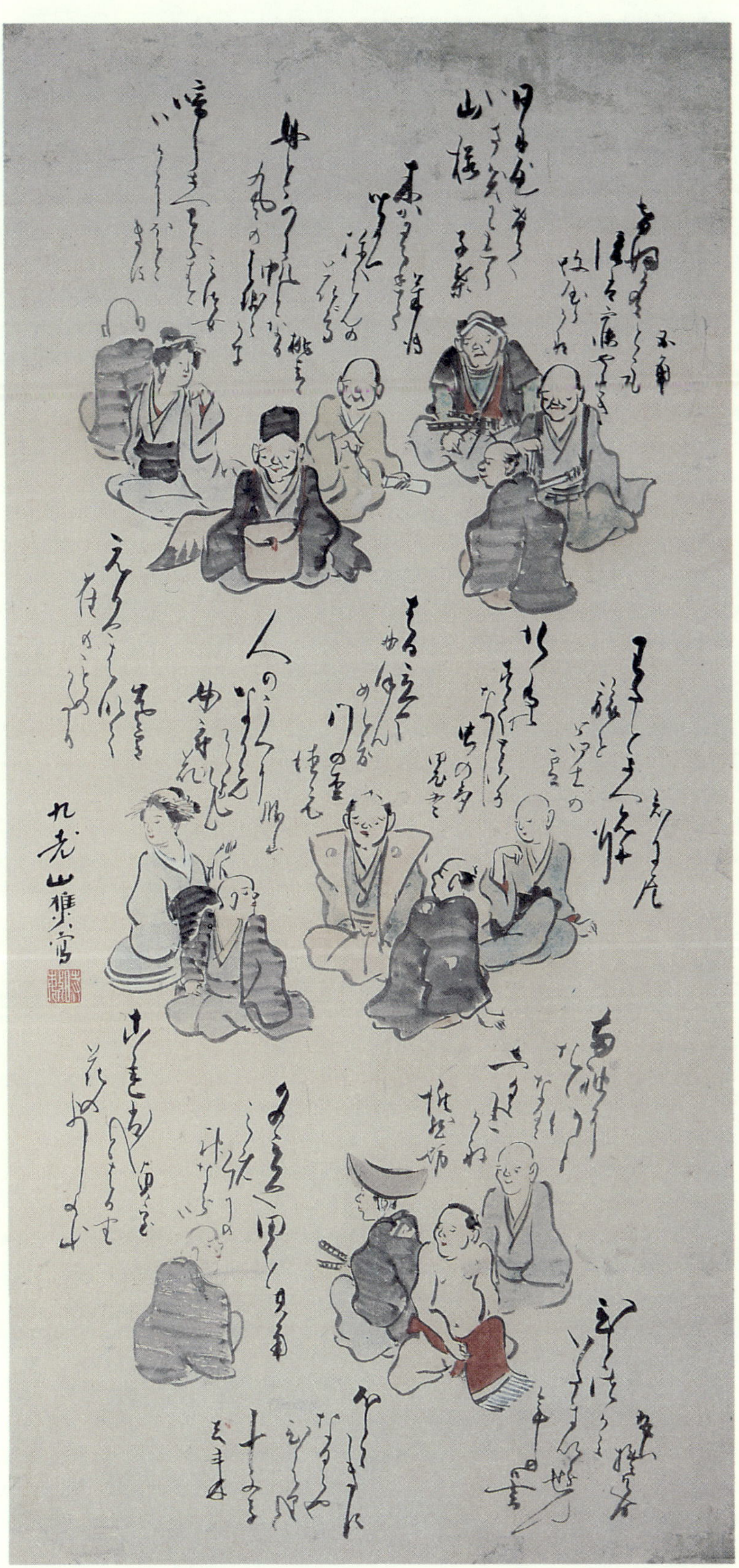

Ki Baitei (1734-1810)
Calligraphy by
Kōnan Setsuko (n.d.)
Thirty Figures
(detail of left panel)
Ink and color on paper;
two panels, each
68 1/4 x 35 1/2 inches
Shōka Collection
Cat. No. 15

HAIGA AND JAPANESE ART

A BRIEF HISTORY OF HAIGA

The first haiga appeared almost as soon as haiku emerged as a distinct poetic tradition in Japan. This is because, in contrast to the more romantic and elegant poetry and painting of the past, haiku and haiga are both forms of expression stemming from direct observation of everyday life. Since they are both created with the same brush and ink, adding an image to a haiku poem was such a natural activity that there is no direct evidence of its first occurrence.

Among early haiku masters, the poet who most often painted haiga was Nonoguchi Ryūho (1595-1669), who is said to have studied painting with the famous artist Kano Tan'yū (1602-1674). Ryūho is sometimes cited as the originator of haiga because his verses are so often accompanied by images. He also wrote on one of his later scrolls that around the age of sixty he began a new practice of painting, although whether or not he specifically meant haiga is not clear.

In most of Ryūho's works, there is more text than just the haiku poem, and the calligraphy is not as visually integrated with the image as in most later haiga. Instead, his introductions and poems often remain somewhat separate from the painting, such as at the top of a hanging scroll or on the side of a horizontal format. Nevertheless, Ryūho's deft paintings add to his poems an element of unpretentious visual delight that fully expresses the haiga spirit.

Although he enjoyed painting haiga, Ryūho considered himself primarily a poet. Like many other haiku masters (and Zen monks), he wrote a death verse at the end of his life. His final haiku, which he carved onto his own memorial stone shortly before he died, demonstrates how he understood his death in terms of poetry; he takes two of the most common haiku themes and suggests that there is one more:

Tsuki yuki no	This world of moonlight
sankume o ima	and snow — now I know what
shiru yo kana	the third line must be

Other early haiku poets also created haiga, although less frequently than Ryūho. The famous novelist Ihara Saikaku (1642-1693) was a well-known haiku poet in the earlier part of his career, and several of his delightful small paintings are graced with his own verses. His creativity as a poet was immense; he once composed sixteen thousand haiku in a single day and night, just to see if it were possible. However, after his novels became extremely popular, he generally gave up composing poems and haiku-paintings.

Haiga, like haiku itself, became a major form of artistic expression with Matsuo Bashō. His modest paintings do not seek to impress viewers with technical prowess, bright colors or bold brushwork, but they set the tone for most haiga that was to follow. Because the images are minimal, they are easy to underestimate at first glance, but they add significantly to the mood by underscoring the imagery of the poems, sometimes adding new layers of meaning (Cat. No. 1). The depth that Bashō gave to haiku poetry also added new resonance to haiku painting, and from this time on, the finest haiga could take an honored place in the world of Japanese art.

Near the end of his life, Bashō wrote that he learned painting from his poetry pupil Morikawa Kyoriku (1656-1715). However, they met only a few years before Bashō died, and the master had already been painting haiga for some years. Kyoriku, who was a skilled artist, probably encouraged and influenced Bashō's final paintings, which are his finest. In return, Bashō must have imparted to Kyoriku not only the methods of haiku, but also a deep aesthetic spirit, since Kyoriku's own haiga are more evocative and focused than his earlier paintings. The two also created a number of cooperative haiga, with paintings by Kyoriku and inscribed poems by Bashō (Cat. Nos. 2 and 3).

Many pupils and followers of Bashō continued his lead in haiga as well as haiku, each adding an individual voice. Kyoriku painted in a modified Kano School style that he had learned from study with Kano Yasunobu (1613-1685). In contrast, Bashō's highly admired haiku pupil, Enomoto Kikaku (1661-1707), showed a special talent for adding extremely lively calligraphy to minimalist images, creating seemingly innocuous paintings in which the underlying flavor is especially pungent (Cat. No. 4). Other followers of the Bashō tradition such as the monk Kakujō (1664-1747), the Ise poet Nakagawa Otsuyu (1675-1739), and the nun Kaga no Chiyo (1703-1775) were also gifted in combining verbal and visual images that offer multiple layers of meaning. Of the three, Kakujō was the most dramatic, adding small but powerfully brushed images to his haiku (Cat. No. 5). Otsuyu was more painterly, utilizing varied tones of ink to create images that blend subtly with his poems (Cat. No. 6). Chiyo, however, was the most lyrical, and the most sophisticated in joining poetry and painting through the unifying element of calligraphy (Cat. No. 7).

In the later eighteenth century, the samurai-poet Yokoi Yayū (1702-1783) became famous for further developing Bashō's literary tradition of *haibun* (haiku poetry combined with prose). Yayū also frequently enjoyed painting haiga of subtle vigor (Cat. No. 8). However, by the late eighteenth century there was a constant battle to keep the Bashō tradition alive and vigorous in the face of pervading tendencies towards wit and cleverness. One poet who resisted these trends and also enjoyed creating lively haiga was Miura Chora (1729-1780), who lived and worked in Ise Province. His haiga have a special charm that stems from his freedom of spirit and unconventional personality (Cat. No. 9). Takebe Ayatari (1719-1774) was also an unconventional poet, excelling in various literary styles as well as painting both elaborate Chinese-style landscapes and much simpler and more relaxed haiga (Cat. No. 10).

The poet-artist who did the most to revive the Bashō approach to poetry in the late eighteenth century was Yosa Buson; he is now considered the second great master in the world of haiku. Buson also became an important painter in the Chinese-style literati tradition, and he is the only artist to be included in surveys both of great poets and of great painters in Japanese history.

Buson's paintings go well beyond haiga, including elaborate bird-and-flower works as well as literati landscapes. However, his haiga are often considered the finest paintings in the haiku text-image tradition (Cat. Nos. 11 and 12). In comparision with most earlier poet-artists, Buson tended to give more space and attention to the images in his haiga, and the great fluency of his brushwork is always apparent. Some of his scrolls go beyond the simplicity and modesty established by Bashō, turning haiga into a more purely painterly medium.

While earlier haiku-painters such as Ryūho and Kyoriku had been influenced by the Kano School style, Buson took haiga into a literati phase of development, in which a relaxed calligraphic style replaces the more descriptive brushwork of the Kano tradition. Longer, curving lines enliven the human figures, and other subjects are often suggested rather than defined. Buson's chief pupils Matsumura Goshun (1752-1811) and Ki Baitei (1734-1810) followed his lead in haiga, most often painting figures such as famous haiku poets. Of the two, Goshun's brushwork is somewhat more polished (Cat. No. 13), while Baitei's is more vigorous (Cat. Nos. 14 and 15). However, midway through his painting career, Goshun came under the influence of the naturalistic painter Maruyama Ōkyo (1733-1795) and changed his style to a softer and more impressionistic naturalism. Since Goshun's studio was on Shijō (4th Avenue) in Kyoto, his new style was called "Shijō," and eventually the combined style became known as "Maruyama-Shijō."

Goshun's work had a strong influence on later artists, so in the early nineteenth century the mainstream of haiga, at least when created by professional painters, changed once again, this time from literati to Maruyama-Shijō school influence. The haiku painting of a crow by Yamaguchi Soken (1759-1818) is a clear example of Maruyama-Shijō techniques, including the use of broad bands of grey ink from a flat brush (see Cat. No. 17) rather than the more linear and calligraphic brushwork of the literati masters. A few artists of the Rimpa (decorative) school also created haiga, notably the cultivated aesthete Sakai Hōitsu (1761-1828), as seen in Cat. Nos. 42 and 43.

Nineteenth-century haiga can be divided into two categories: those by poets and those by painters. But the divisions are by no means clear in every case. Takebe Sōchō (Cat. Nos. 18-33) represents both groups, the poets who painted and the professional painters who created haiga. Although Sōchō was primarily a poet, he also studied painting and became skilled enough to create not only haiga, but also paintings with or without inscriptions in a variety of styles.

When Sōchō created haiga, he may have been influenced by the style of Buson and his followers, but many of his images seem more spontaneous and less purely painterly. Nevertheless, his artistic skills allowed him to depict a number of subjects, using relaxed brushwork in his haiga and more detailed and elaborate techniques in his other paintings. The same division can be seen in the works of Ayatari, who painted very simply in his haiga and much more fully when depicting landscapes in literati style. It becomes clear through examining Sōchō's and Ayatari's works that haiga had come to be understood as a special style of art, in which more modest compositions, fewer and looser brush lines, less color, and more humor are seen than in most other forms of Japanese painting.

Other haiga of the early and middle nineteenth century tend to divide more clearly into poet-paintings and artist-paintings. The third of the great haiku masters, Kobayashi Issa, was the ultimate poet-as-painter. His haiga seem totally unskillful, with only a few amateurish lines defining his subjects (Cat. No. 34). Yet his work conveys great emotive expression. Is this despite his seemingly clumsy painting technique? Or because of it? In any case, the amount of feeling that Issa invested in his poems is also clearly expressed in his haiga, giving them an intimate and powerful force that is only enhanced by their simplicity.

Several other leading poets of Issa's era also painted extremely simply, including the Nagoya doctor Inoue Shirō and his friend Fujimori Sōbaku (1758-1821). Shirō experimented with many different subjects, including figures, birds, and landscapes (Cat. Nos. 35-37), while Sōbaku adopted a bold and somewhat sardonic style in depicting figures (Cat. No. 38). Most of their haiga, like Issa's, avoids the use of color, and their restraint with the brush makes their paintings even more effective. In contrast, professional painters such as Suzuki Nanrei (1775-1844) and Nakamura Hōchū (active c. 1790-1813) tend to use color a good deal of the time, and to fill their compositions with highly skilled and sometimes dramatic brushwork (see Cat. Nos. 39-41). Nevertheless, they maintain a good deal of the haiku spirit; in comparison with their other paintings, their haiga are not as fully elaborated, and tend to be restrained and relaxed in spirit.

Most haiga in this century have followed the lead of earlier traditions, with a slight tendency to echo modern trends in Japanese painting by elaborating the forms and filling the compositions. Again there is some division between professional painters and poet-painters. The former, such as Kawabata Gyokushō (1842-1913, Cat. No. 48) and Hayashi Buntō (1882-1966, Cat. No. 49), usually follow the naturalistic tradition of Maruyama-Shijō painting. This style, with various admixtures, became known in the twentieth century as *Nihonga,* (literally "Japanese painting"), and it has been very influential throughout the century. Haiku poets who paint, on the other hand, have continued to produce extremely simple haiga such as the snail crawling up the side of a scroll (Cat. No. 51) by Hattori Kan'unshi (1883-?) .

Haiga are still being produced in Japan, and there are even "how-to" books that tell amateurs how to add images to their haiku poems. The future direction of haiga is uncertain, however, since it depends on the future of haiku itself. At the moment, haiku is still a widely practiced form of verse, but it must contend with powerful influences that lead potential poets away from nature, away from an extraordinary awareness of the seasons, and away from the observation of minute but flavorful moments of daily life. Instead of the traditional cycles of rural life, there is now a pervading focus on urban existence, with its stress on products and possessions. Japanese, like Americans, are also being deluged with mass entertainment through radio, photography, recordings, television, film, and video. We can only hope that both haiku poetry and haiga will continue to serve as a counterweight to the pressures of the modern world.

HAIGA SUBJECT MATTER AND STYLE

Almost any subject can be painted in haiga, including the traditional figures, landscapes, and bird-and-flower themes that have long been portrayed in other forms of Japanese art. However, one feature that often distinguishes haiga is its focus upon a single, often unnoticed or dismissed subject, such as a few rocks in a dried-out stream bed (Cat. No. 12) or a discarded melon skin (Cat. No. 4). Just as haiku poetry pays close attention to the least of earthly objects and creatures, so does haiga picture them with a few deft strokes of the brush.

In many haiga, the image in the painting is also the subject, or one of the subjects, of the poem. In others, however, the main theme of the poem is not directly shown. For example, one of the recurring subjects in this book is moon-viewing, which appears in many guises by various artists; in each case the painting brings forth an essential element to enhance the spirit behind the poem. Three artists depict the full moon of autumn. Ayatari paints it in the upper left corner of his haiga and allows the poem to occupy the rest of the space (Cat. No. 10). Chōkōbō Roshōan (1797-1875) similarly depicts the moon in the same upper corner, but does not mention it in his poem. More boldly, the Zen Master Nantembō (1839-1925) emblazons the circle of the moon at the top of his long hanging scroll, inviting the viewer to "try to catch it" (Cat. No. 47).

In contrast, Sōchō paints one figural work on which Sōkan's haiku about the moon has been inscribed (Cat. No. 28) and two works with his own haiku about the late autumn moon (Cat. No. 23 and 24), but in none of these haiga is the moon itself painted. Is it visible to the imaginations of those who read the poems? Only in his pair of screens does Sōchō actually paint the moon (Cat. No. 18), and there it is a crescent moon rather than the more famous full moon of mid-autumn. Even more subtly, Inoue Shirō uses only one stoke of the brush to suggest the mountain behind which the moon rises, and that becomes the entire image (Cat. No. 37). Yet when his calligraphy of the character "moon" rises over the mountain, the word becomes an image, and the image a word. In Shirō's haiga of a cuckoo, the moon is again suggested by its written character, but moonlight also seems to pervade the silk background of the painting (Cat. No. 38).

Each of these poet-artists creates a different picture of the moon in both haiku and painting, and each reinforces his poetic vision by blending the arts into a unified expression. There are a number of other haiga in which the painting does not directly depict what is stated in the poem, but adds new imagery. For example, Buntō's haiku poem tells us only that shops at the beach are all boarded up while insects chirp (Cat. No. 49). But his painting shows us a *kappa,* a mischievous creature who adds a whole new layer of meaning to the haiga. He is lonely, but we humans may prefer a lonely *kappa* to one who is bedeviling us, and this gives Buntō's work a delightful humor that his poem by itself lacks. Similarly, Gyokushō's haiku does not mention Nihonbashi, but his picture of that famous bridge leading in and out of Tokyo adds a significant image to his poem about a New Year's banquet (Cat. No. 48).

A third subject for haiga does not deal with the poem at all, but instead consists of portraits of poets. Of course, poet-painting was nothing new to Japan. Paintings of famous *waka* poets had been created for hundreds of years, especially by artists associated with the court who featured delicate brushwork, detailed compositions, and bright colors. Images of the "thirty-six" or "one hundred" great *waka* masters became so popular that such portraits even appeared on card and shell games, where participants had to match the poets with their most famous verses.

Partly in emulation and partly in parody of this tradition, portraits began to be painted of haiku poets, but without such delicate colors and refined brushwork. Instead, the haiku masters were shown very simply in free brushwork, using ink or light colors. Rather than appearing as noble monks, refined courtiers, and exquisite court ladies, they are shown as everyday people. Even Bashō, the most frequently depicted haiku master, is sometimes portrayed dozing or staring into space, as can be seen in works by Baitei, Sōchō, and Nanrei (see Cat. Nos. 14, 32, and 39).

Whatever the subject, haiga were painted by poets and artists who felt that words alone did not convey all the layers of meaning in haiku. In the best haiga, a concentration of verbal and pictorial vision is created that comes primarily from a heightened awareness of nature, including human nature. This awareness is best expressed by suggestion rather than full definition. As the scholar John Rosenfield has suggested about Japanese art, the stronger the power of poetic inspiration, the less need for pictorial detail. What unites the haiga of poet-artists, from Bashō in the seventeenth century to Shimomura Izan in the twentieth, is the simple, direct, and unpretentious style of painting that suggests more meanings than it defines.

Takebe Sōchō (1761-1814)
Portrait of Bashō, 1892
(detail)
Woodblock print, mounted on scroll,
24 3/4 x 12 inches
Masuda Shōzaburō Collection, Tokyo
Cat. No. 32

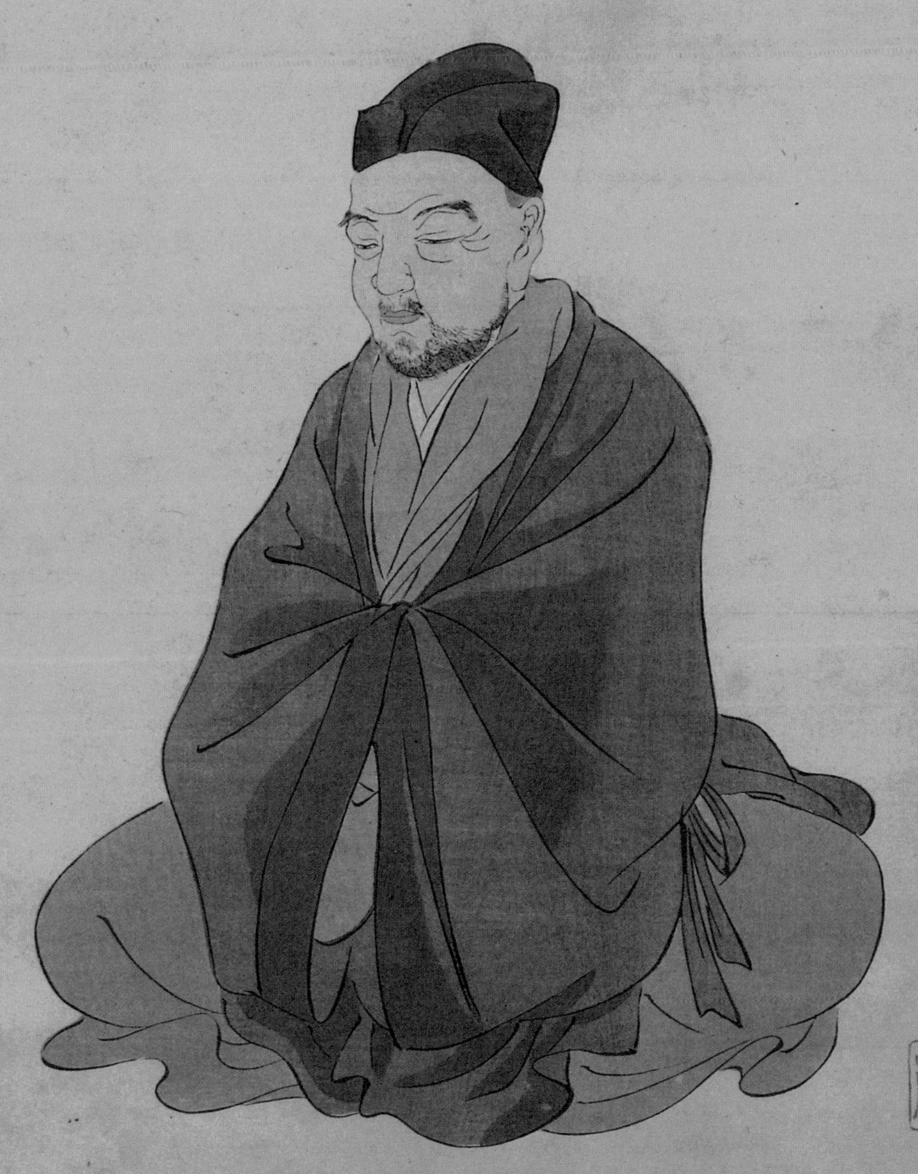
築兆建部英親謹畫
松甫

TAKEBE SŌCHŌ (1761-1814) *by Fumiko Y. Yamamoto*

Kono michi ya	On this road
yuku hito nashi ni	no one goes
aki no kure	autumn eve

Thus Matsuo Bashō sang in the seventeenth century. Although the seventeen-syllable haiku (also called *haikai* and *hokku)* was already recognized as a poetic form in Bashō's time, his mission to elevate the haiku to a highly artistic genre was not an easy one. Ever driven by his desire for perfection in this brief form, Bashō saw himself as the lonely traveler in this haiku, which he composed in his last days. He stands alone on the road, and his vision as a poet haunts him to the end:

Tabi ni yande	Taken ill on a journey
yume wa kareno o	my dreams roam around
kake meguru	over the withered field

Roughly a century later, Takebe Sōchō sees another traveler in his haiku:

Tabi hitori	Alone on journey
hihara hihara to	"hihara, hihara"
kari ga naku	a wild goose cries

The season is the same and the traveler is again by himself. Yet the effects in Bashō's first haiku and Sōchō's are quite different. Sōchō's traveler is not completely alone. He finds a sympathetic agent in nature, which accompanies him, while the onomatopoeia adds an almost droll peacefulness to the scene. The desolation and tension in Bashō's haiku are replaced by Sōchō's enjoyment of the setting. The old master's struggle between poetic vision and physical limitation in his haiku gives way to the later poet's relaxed feeling of leisure. Sōchō is not racing against time, and he prefers to step aside from his daily life to enjoy his discoveries along the way. Haiku was not his sole way of life, but one of many forms of artistic expression by which he savored existence in the here and now. And this is the poetic sensitivity shared by many of the sophisticated urban poets in the early nineteenth century when Sōchō was active.

Sōchō was born in Edo to the well-respected Yamamoto family, which had accompanied the shogun Tokugawa Ieyasu (1542-1616) when he moved to Edo in the late sixteenth century. The Yamamoto family occupied the hereditary position of *nanushi* (head) of several townships in the Nihonbashi district of the city. According to the research of the collector-scholar Masuda Shōzaburō, Sōchō's family also served the Tokugawa government as *bakurōgashira,* who provided laborers and relay horses. Sōchō's father was the famous calligrapher Yamamoto Ryūsai, who was also a haiku poet. Ryūsai's wealth and love for art provided him ample occasion to associate with men of culture of the time, including Kameda Bōsai (1752-1826), a well-known Confucian scholar and literary man who took Ryūsai's daughter as his wife. It is easy to imagine that Sōchō's artistic inclinations were nurtured early in this family background.

Born when Ryūsai was fifty-two, Sōchō must have had a great respect for his father, sometimes using a seal reading "Shōho" which Ryūsai had used. His memory of his father is also recorded in his haiku. The opening panel in his *byōbu* (pair of 12-panel screens, see Cat. No. 18) states that, when visiting Takasago in Harima (present day Hyōgo Prefecture), Sōchō came across a calligraphy done by his late father. Sōchō commemorates the event with a haiku:

Takasago ni
oya no sho mo ari
fude hajime

At Takasago
my father's calligraphy —
first brushwork of the year

Sōchō celebrates the joining of his father's memory with the auspicious place of Takasago, where a shrine is associated with the image of an old couple who symbolize happy marriage and longevity. The painting shows Sōchō's first brushstrokes of the year, and simply depicts a branch of pine and a broom used by the old couple as they sweep the white sand under the evergreen pine tree at the Takasago shrine.

In addition to his father's instruction in calligraphy and haiku, Sōchō studied haiku under Kaya Shirao (1738-91), as well as painting under Sakurai Keigetsu (dates unknown) and others. Sōchō became a talented and versatile artist, and his extant works show his various painting styles. He also mastered the tea ceremony and flower arranging, often regarded as necessary artistic qualifications to be considered a man of refinement. Sōchō was later adopted by the Fujisawa family in Senju in Edo, and was commonly called Fujisawa Heiemon. His early haiku name was Ōjaku, but after he retired to the area called Sekiya in Senju, a location west of the Sumida River that was deeply loved by many poets, he was called Sekiya Sōchō. His other haiku names include Saiō and Shūkōan. Well-respected as a poet-painter, Sōchō was named as one of the three leading Edo haiku masters of the time, along with Suzuki Michihiko (1757-1819) and Natsume Seibi (1749-1816). Sōchō also compiled over thirty haiku-related books during his lifetime, the most famous one being *Sekiyajō (Sekiya Booklet),* a collection of haiku by various poets that was edited by Sōchō in 1802 when he stayed at Kakitsubo in Osaka.

Traditional *waka* often reflected the close relationship between poets, such as the verse sent by a man to his beloved and her reply to him, especially after a night's courtship. The rapport and exchanges of sentiment between two people were extended to encompass several poets when the practice of composing linked verse (*renga)* became popular. Haiku, which was originally the starting verse of the *renga,* perhaps carried remnants of that camaraderie, and the feeling of sharing that was fostered in haiku composed among kindred spirits contributed much to the frequent gatherings of poets and artists during Sōchō's time. The artists challenged and inspired one another, and they often combined their talents by joining together on the same scroll or other work of art.

Sōchō's artistic friends were many. He knew Natsume Seibi well, and through Seibi he met the major haiku master Kobayashi Issa (1763-1827). Among Sōchō's close poet-painter acquaintances, perhaps most well known were Kameda Bōsai (1752-1826) and Sakai Hōitsu (1761-1828). In Sōchō's posthumous collection of haiku, *Sobakari (Reaping of Buckwheat,* 1817), both Bōsai and Hōitsu offer introductions. Bōsai praises Sōchō as a man who "loved sake and loved guests. When he had money in his hand, he had no hesitation in scattering it quickly; he was gracious." Hōitsu, in his turn, fondly recalls his association with Sōchō: "Composing a haiku on flowers or on the moon, he would show it to me. Writing a haiku, I also asked his opinion. . . . When I painted, he would give me a title. When he painted, I added words. When he raised his cup, I ate rice cakes." Sōchō's gentle and sensitve haiku and lively accompanying paintings were created in this cultural milieu of the celebration of the goodness of life.

The four seasons regulate haiku. They are the background against which each poet sings a unique discovery of the moment in this eternal flow. Let us accompany Sōchō in his seasonal journey. His *byōbu* covers the twelve months in order, beginning with the new year (see Cat. No. 18). The second panel describes Sekiya, where Sōchō lived "only one hundred steps from the Sumida River. It is a beautiful area, famous for the moon and snow." After composing three haiku describing spring with the image of cherry blossoms, Sōchō adds an historical layer to the panel by depicting Ariwara Narihira, a ninth-century courtier who immortalized the name of the Sumida river by the *waka* he composed at the riverside, full of longing and sentiment for his loved one left in Kyoto.

It was a sad occasion for Narihira, but what Sōchō's painting evokes is a gentle recollection of the elegance long past.

Sōchō's haiga handscroll of 1799, painted at the temple Zenkō-ji, also depicts spring at Sekiya (see Cat. No. 25), where two huts by the river are drawn with simple lines. After two haiku referring to plum blossoms, Sōchō brings in a warbler, the bird often associated with plum flowers. This warbler, however, is not displaying its usual poise on the branch:

Uguisu no yane yori oriru hatake kana	The warbler comes down from the rooftop to the field

The connection between the poem and the soft line of the thatched roofs is achieved in the viewer's mental picture.

Spring always brings hope for new growth. Perhaps Sōchō was traveling when a peculiar sound caught his attention:

Ta ya kaesu hetara hetara to tani no soko	Plowing over the paddy? "plish plash" valley bottom

A farmer is busy preparing his field for spring planting. The sound reaching Sōchō tells him that the paddy is wet. To capture the humor in the sound, Sōchō paints a long lotus root and several *kuwai* arrowhead bulbs; both grow in water (see Cat. No. 19). Sōchō's calligraphy waves like a lotus root, and the haiga is an intriguing harmony of the long, the narrow, the pointed and the round.

Two haiku that follow this poem in Sōchō's book *Sobakari* express the human reaction to animals. The working farmer is not oblivious to the wild fox, which is believed to have bewitching power and has the ability to signal a good harvest. To appeal to the fox, the farmer makes him an offering:

Hatake utsu ya ana no kitsune ni mochi suete	Tilling the fields — and leaving by the foxes' den a rice cake

The cat is a domesticated animal, but despite its close association with humans, its willful behavior makes people suspect its strangeness:

Dokozo de wa baba ni ya naran takerineko	Somewhere it may become a hag — the raging cat

Just as he observes common animals, Sōchō's attention is also given to ordinary plants:

Heta to oku nabe no meguri mo haru no kusa	Slap! I put down a cooking pot amidst the spring grasses

Anything in nature can become poetic inspiration. Wisteria in the late spring is a popular topic in haiku and haiga, as seen in Kaga no Chiyo's poem (Cat. No. 7). Sōchō has a different scrutiny of the flowers:

Fuji saite yuratsuku hashi no sugata kana	Wisteria in bloom — the shape of a swaying bridge

Sōchō's haiku captures the illusory movement of the bridge amid the waving clusters of flowers — a slightly unnerving vision.

When the rice paddies are tilled in early summer, water is drawn into them so that they may be planted:

Hiya hiya to ta ni hashirikomu shimizu kana	Cool, cool running into the rice paddies clear water

Sōchō's use of the onomatopoeia "hiya hiya" and his repitition of the "shi" sound are responses to the freshness of the water and the verdant scenery enveloping the rice fields.

In summer, even pesky mosquitoes become a topic for a haiku:

Susuki kara ka no deru yado ni tomarikeri	From the pampas grass mosquitoes came into the inn where I stayed

The calligraphy on the right starts large, calling the reader's attention to the annoying insects, and then it trails off to lead our eyes to the dominant image on the paper.The room in the modest inn is shared by many travelers (see Cat. No. 26). The mosquito net is not big enough to hold all of them, and some can barely put their heads under it. The air is sultry, but they can spend a night chatting with fellow lodgers. The round shapes of the people's bodies and the circle of the group enhance the feeling that even this wretched lodging can be a place for temporal companionship. Even the baby's tiny round face joins the circle of talk. This loving attention to the small and the modest make haiku and haiga stand apart from the elegant *waka* world.

While Sōchō enjoyed portraying figures such as the gregarious people in the inn, he also created several haiku about the cicada, a summer insect much loved by the Japanese:

Semi naku ya tobashiru taki ni hajikarete	A cicada cries as the gushing waterfall flings it off
Semi no ne ni usugumo kakaru hayashi kana	To the cicada voices a thin cloud hangs over the grove

These haiku suggest the juxtaposition of the sensations of sound and movement. Here Sōchō comes close to the spirit of Bashō in his quiet communion with nature. Yet the two poets' temperaments are different when they picture the "heavenly river" of the Milky Way. Bashō sees:

Araumi ya Sado ni yokotō ama no gawa	The rough sea — stretching over Sado Island the heavenly river

In contrast to Bashō's majestic scene, in which human figures would be dwarfed, Sōchō observes the Japanese conception that night dew can whiten clothing:

Yozarashi no futano hosunari ama no gawa	All through the night underclothes are hung to be bleached — the heavenly river

The whiteness and stretching out of the Milky Way are aligned with the woman's humble undergarments, and Sōchō's "heavenly river" is pulled down to human level.

When Sōchō's observation turns to himself, it becomes humorous:

Oinureba suika ni suberu odori kana	As I get old, slipping on a watermelon rind — my dance

The scene is a blend of self-recognition, good-natured resignation, and gaiety. There is no trace of sentimentality, the enemy of all fine poetry.

The moon in the eighth month is beautiful, yet the moon on the thirteenth night of the ninth month, called the later moon, is even more beautiful in the clear autumn air. A pensive mood accompanies this clear moonlight, which is tremendously appealing to Japanese poets. To this lunar scene, Sōchō adds human interest:

Dore kara to ogi no tonari ya nochi no tsuki	Where did it come from? next to the waterside reeds — late autumn moon

Sōchō did not draw the moon in his haiga (see Cat. No. 23). Instead he magnified the humble water-reeds in soft wet brushwork. And like the moon, his haiku looms above the leaf. His signature delicately perches on the other leaf, like an insect which often adds a melancholy feeling to moon-gazing. Sōchō's human interest is more obvious in another painting with the same haiku (see Cat. No. 24). It was quite a common practice among poets to use the same haiku in different paintings, and here there is no moon, no reeds, but an old couple talking. In *Sobakari,* this haiku has a short foreword stating, "I came to the place called Nakagawa. There was a small house, and as it was tasteful, I peeped in and then. . . ." Perhaps the old couple in the hut are wondering where the moon will come out. The haiku and paintings invite multiple interpretations.

The autum moon entertains the poet, but autumn also brings the waning of nature's lifeforce. Sōchō's ears discern the change:

Fukinureba hōki ni naku ya kirigirisu	As the wind blows — from inside the broom a katydid chirps

The insect's sound will soon die out, and what will remain are howling gusts of autumn wind.

In late autumn, the tobacco leaves are ready to be shipped:

Tabako-ni no mare ni hitome mo kareno kana	Tobacco packs seldom seen by people — withered fields

We have already seen desolate fields reflected in Bashō's dying eyes. Here in Sōchō's haiku, humans are still engaging in their activities (see Cat. No. 21). Tobacco, a luxury item, is supported by the hard labor of working people and animals. Both a man with a stick and a horse that seems to have its own will are full of life and present a contrast to the quiet haiku. This is the joy of haiga, which never ceases to stimulate the viewer's imagination.

In the last scene of Sōchō's 1807 handscroll, two figures are crouching in front of a hearth with two big cooking pots, preparing food for the new year (see Cat. No. 18). Round *mochi* cakes seem to be waiting on a shelf for the coming of the celebration. The scene may be a depiction of a kitchen at Zenkō-ji. It is a busy time of year, yet people, even monks, are having a good time:

Toshi kurenu	At year's end
hi o taku ni sae	even making a fire
omoshiromi	is delightful

Their minds are already filled with excitement for the new year.

Sōchō is certainly aware of the severity of winter, as he tells us:

Yukiakari	Snow sheen
akaruki neya wa	lights up the bed chamber —
mata samushi	still cold

The light itself congeals into coldness. Yet what Sōchō likes to describe more is the enjoyment he finds in this evanescent "floating world." People usually bustle around to finish everything before a new year comes. But for Sōchō, who retired to Sekiya, even the end of a year offered a carefree time of leisure (see Cat. No. 22). Sōchō sings:

Waga io wa	My hermitage
Yoshiwara kasumu	the Yoshiwara haze —
shiwasu kana	last month of the year

The accompanying picture of a samurai is perhaps triggered by a common expression *shiwasu rōnin* (masterless samurai at the end of the year) who has no business to take care of at this busy time. The original phrase refers to poverty and rootlessness, but what Sōchō evokes in the image and poem is lightheartedness; the figure with a hat on his head and a fan in his hand is casually strolling back to his hut. Being from a respected *nanushi* family, Sōchō was perhaps allowed to wear a sword, and this man possibly embodies Sōchō's mental image of himself, if not a lifelike representation. The lone man's relaxed posture, the soft brushwork, the waving reeds, and the spatial extension all echo the poet's freedom of spirit.

Sōchō's *byōbu,* which had started with the auspicious legendary figures at Takasago shrine, ends with another image of a shrine. It indicates that when Sōchō came to the forest of Ikuta (situated in present day Kobe), he thought of the history of the Ikuta shrine and composed a haiku:

Koyuki seyo	Let the light snow fall,
kasa kite mawan	I'll dance with my sedge hat
kami no mae	in front of the god

The man, perhaps Sōchō himself, concludes the *byōbu* with his solitary dance. Yet his figure, facing to the right, suggests that he is related to the rest of the panels: the scene is not one of finality, but presents a sense of the ending of one seasonal cycle. Sōchō's poetic season ever starts anew.

1. Matsuo Bashō (1644-1694)

Gate and Banana Plants

Ink and color on paper, 38 3/8 x 11 5/8 (97.3 x 29.7)
Idemitsu Museum of Arts, Tokyo

Bashō is acknowledged as the greatest master of haiku in Japanese history; his poems, prose, and haiku journeys such as *Narrow Road to the Interior* are frequently translated into English. However, his paintings and calligraphy are less well known outside Japan. Perhaps this is because the qualities of modesty and simplicity that are so admired in haiga have not yet been fully appreciated in the art world of the West.

It has long been believed in East Asia that calligraphy reveals the inner character of the writer; combined with painting, it can present a visual record of the human spirit. Neither Bashō's calligraphy nor his painting are flamboyant. Instead of proclaiming his technical prowess, they seem simple, casual, amateur, and almost childlike. If we remember that the word "amateur" comes from the word for love, we can understand how Bashō has no need to seem bold, dramatic, skilled, or professional. Instead, he writes and paints just enough to suggest an image that can resonate in our own eyes, mind, and spirit.

Minomushi no	Come and listen
ne o kiki ni koyo	to the sound of the bagworms —
kusa no io	grass hut

This haiku was first written by Bashō to his pupil Sodō (1642-1716), inviting him to visit for an autumn poetry party. The painting adds significantly to the meaning of the words, and becomes a form of self-portrait. Bashō's name literally means "banana plant," and he is strongly identified with his hermitage, "Bashō-an," where he planted the banana plant given to him by one of his pupils. But he does not picture the hut itself. By painting the gateway to his home, Bashō invites us to visit him through his art, if we can fulfill one condition — we must be able to hear the sound of bagworms, which are silent.

Note: Dimensions given are of the image exclusive of the mounting, height before width, inches before centimeters.

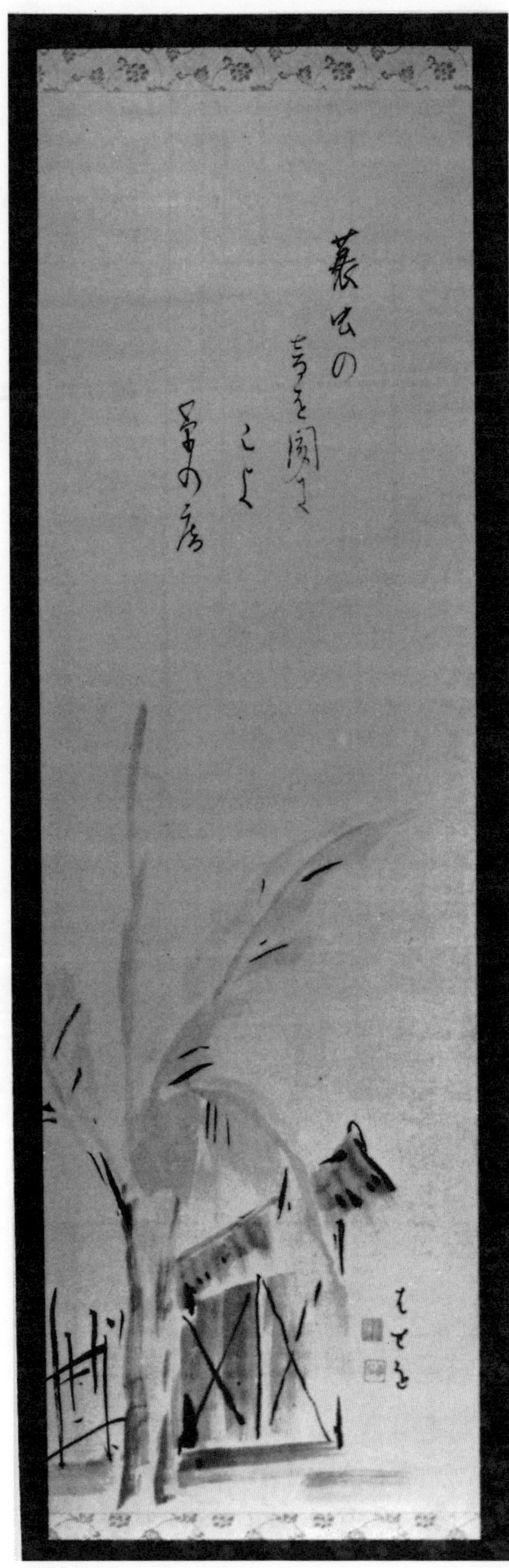

2. Morikawa Kyoriku, also known as Kyoroku (1656-1715)
Inscription by Matsuo Bashō (1644-1694)

Sparrows

Ink and color on paper, 11 1/4 x 30 1/16 (28.6 x 76.5)
Yabumoto Collection, Tokyo

A samurai from Hikone in Shiga, Kyoriku studied painting with the professional master Kano Yasunobu (1613-1685) and later served as an artist to the *Daimyō* (Lord) of Hikone. Kyoriku became a poetry pupil of Bashō in 1692, and when he returned to Hikone after his master's death in 1694, he taught and wrote extensively about the Bashō haiku tradition.

Bashō wrote in his farewell words to Kyoriku, entitled *The Rustic Gate,* that Kyoriku loved poetry because of painting, and painting because of poetry, studying them both for a single purpose and forming an admirable combination of the two arts. Bashō particularly praised Kyoriku's paintings, which he claimed were done with a skill and depth much greater than his own. The two collaborated on several scrolls, for which Kyoriku added paintings to haiku by Bashō. This scroll features five poems about sparrows in Bashō's modest, gently flowing calligraphy. The second poem, when it was published, included Bashō's introduction, "If we look serenely, we can see that everything is at peace with itself."

Nabatake ni hanamigao naru suzume kana	In the mustard fields making flower-viewing faces — sparrows
Hana ni asobu abu na kurai so tomosuzume	Sparrow friends — please don't eat the horsefly playing in the blossoms
Suzumego ya koe nakikawasu nezumi no su	Baby sparrows — exchanging their cheeps with a nest of mice
Ine suzume cha no ki batake ya nige dokoro	Rice-field sparrows can escape from hunters in the groves of tea
Sekizoro o suzume no warau detachi kana	Year-end mummers are a sight to make the sparrows laugh

Kyoriku's two sparrows circle and call to each other, perhaps like Bashō and Kyoriku in this happy collaboration.

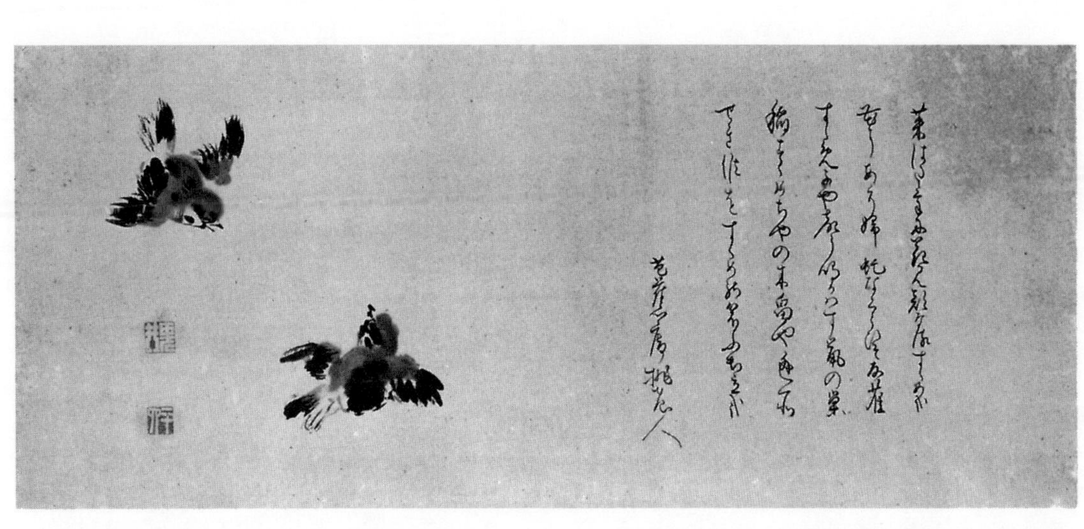

3. Morikawa Kyoriku (1656-1715)

Inscription by Matsuo Bashō (1644-1694)

Crow on a Withered Branch

Ink on paper, 42 1/8 x 12 1/4 (107 x 31.2)
Idemitsu Museum of Arts, Tokyo

One of Bashō's most famous poems is here masterfully visualized by Kyoriku, who freely based his image upon a celebrated painting by the Chinese Zen monk Mu Ch'i (1177-1239). Kyoriku's crow is mournfully huddled up against the cold, his eyes and beak barely visible. This exemplifies a Japanese perception of autumn: dark, sere, chilly, and lonely. To enhance the emotional focus, the tilting oval of the crow's body creates a strong black accent against the more delicate calligraphy above and spiky twigs below. Bashō inscribed his poem in a three-line composition that echoes the descending rhythms of the painting:

Kara eda ni	Crow perching
karasu no tomarikeri	on a withered branch —
aki no kure	autumn evening

The largest word in Bashō's calligraphy is *aki* (autumn), which begins the final, lowest line of calligraphy on the left. This shows that Bashō too felt the strongest stress in this haiga should be the desolate feeling of the season that Kyoriku captured so well in his painting.

For lovers of haiku, one fascinating question about Bashō's poem has long been whether there is one crow or many crows, perched on a single or multiple branches. Since the Japanese language does not distinguish singular or plural here, the poem could be translated:

Crows perching
on withered branches —
autumn evening

However, since Bashō inscribed his haiku on this painting of a single crow on a single branch, can't we conclude that the singlular is correct? Perhaps, but Bashō had previously written the same poem on a painting of many crows on many branches. To confuse the issue further, even earlier in his career Bashō had painted one crow on one branch with this poem. Unless we want to believe that Bashō kept changing his mind, we must realize that both readings are possible, and that Bashō may have wished that we not be limited to a single interpretation of his poem.

かれえだに
からすのとまりたるや
秋のくれ

芭蕉桃青

三杏丹許六画

4. Enomoto Kikaku, also known as Takarai (1661-1707)

Melon Skin

Ink on paper, 12 1/4 x 17 1/2 (31 x 44.4)
Shōka Collection

Of all his many pupils and followers, Bashō seems to have been most fond of Kikaku, despite their differences in personality. Where Bashō was serious, Kikaku was lighthearted, and his poems are highly admired for their *karumi,* or lightness of touch.

The son of a physician, Kikaku became Bashō's pupil in his early teens, also studying painting, medicine, Chinese-style poetry, and Confucianism. His spirit was free and bold, and Bashō once criticized Kikaku for trying to find unusual subjects for his haiku, rather than observing everyday objects and events. In this haiga Kikaku depicts the most tawdry of objects, a section of melon rind floating down a stream.

Perhaps no other form of art has such modest ambitions — who but a haiku poet would paint a discarded melon skin? Just like the subject itself, this is a painting that viewers could easily pass by in search of something more rare, grand, and colorful. And yet this unglamorous theme, simply rendered with freely flowing calligraphy, allows Kikaku to express his fresh poetic vision of ordinary life.

Uri no kawa
mizu mo kumode ni
nagarekeri

Melon skin —
spider-legs floating
on the water

The painting helps to illuminate the scene: someone has cut the melon in sections in order to eat its fruit, and now Kikaku shows these sliced sections of skin gradually spreading out and bobbing on the water. But there is more in the poem: *kumode* means spider-legs, but it can mean crosswise or in various directions, so a second translation might be:

Melon skin —
thc water also flowing
in crisscross directions

As we examine the poem, calligraphy, and painting, we can see that this haiga is not as simple as it appears. The water flows, the poem flows, the calligraphy flows, the spider flows, even the melon skin flows; perhaps Kikaku is ultimately suggesting how everyday life, in all its aspects, flows on for us all, whether we notice it or not.

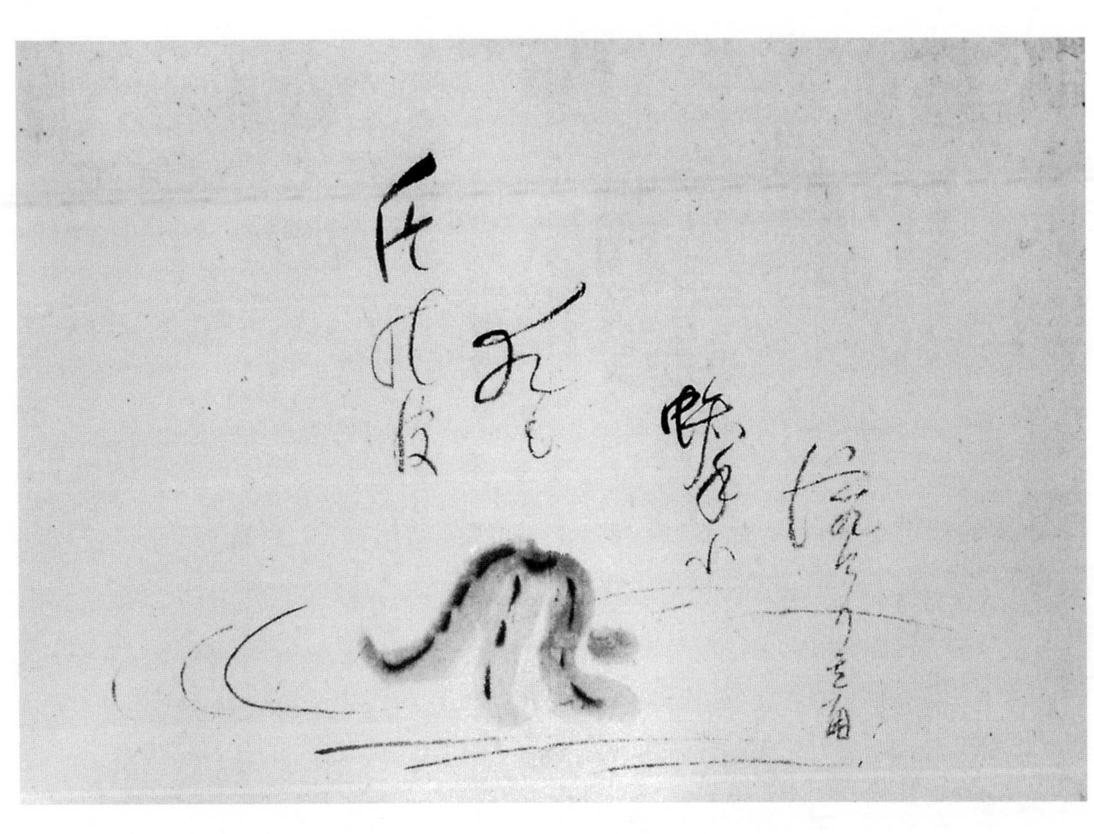

5. Kakujō (1664-1747)

Sailing on the Blue Sea

Ink on paper, 10 1/4 x 14 3/8 (26 x 36.7)
Beckett Collection

Kakujō represents the first generation of haiku poets after Bashō. In Japan, when there is no natural son, the family line is often continued through adoption, and Kakujō was thus adopted by Senna (1651-1723), the haiku poet, painter, and abbot of Honpuku-ji in Shiga Prefecture. It is reported that Bashō often visited Senna at his temple, and may have learned painting from the monk-artist while sharing his knowledge of poetry. From this artistic background, Kakujō grew up to become thirteenth abbot of Honpuku-ji and a noted haiku master himself. Here his poem is largely celebratory:

Aoumi ya	The blue sea —
kyō no suzumi mo	Kyoto's coolness also
iso senri	1000 miles of seashore

Kakujō has painted a figure who may represent Hotei, the god of good fortune, open-mouthed with wonder as he sails in the brisk wind. The composition is masterfully arranged on a strong diagonal with the boat moving rapidly through the space while the calligraphy flutters in the breeze on the right. The round cypher-signature of the artist in the lower right echoes Hotei's open mouth, while the signature above the cypher cleverly reinforces the artist's own name, which literally means "above the corner." But it is the empty space in the center of the format that allows us to enter into the scroll and enjoy the cool breeze for ourselves.

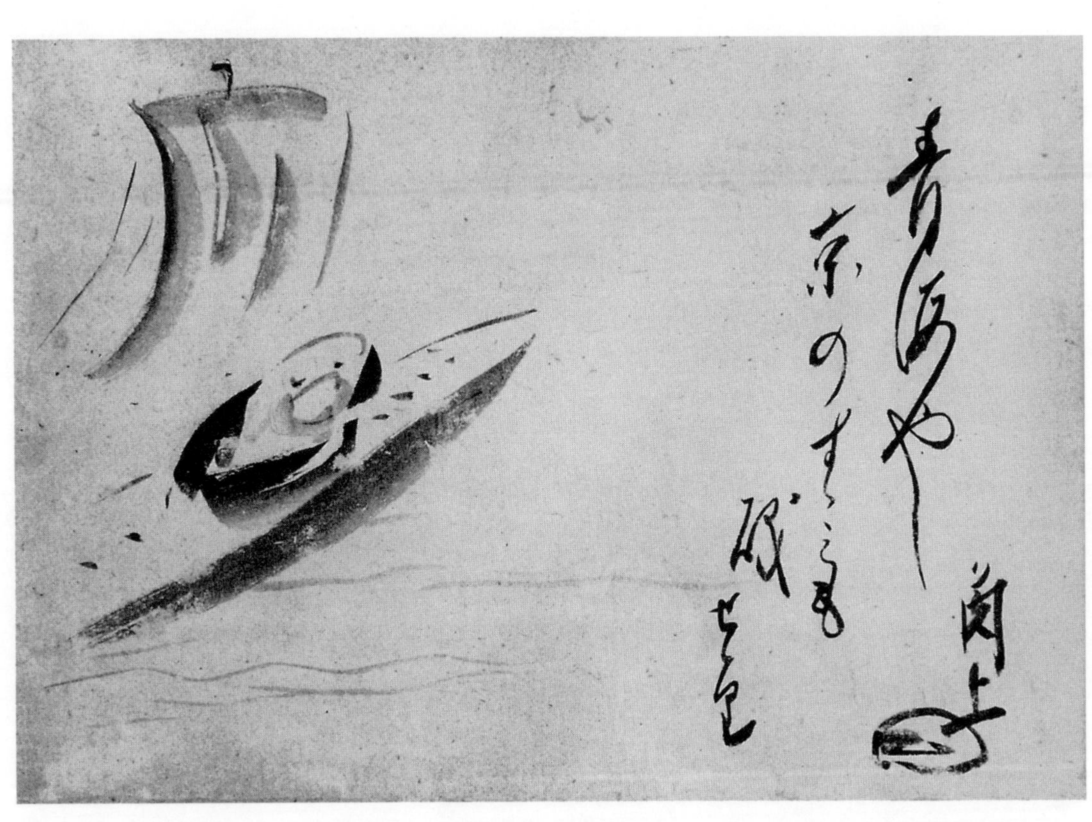

6. Nakagawa Otsuyu, also known as Bakurin (1675-1739)

Deer

Ink on paper, 10 7/8 x 14 3/4 (27.7 x 37.6)
Beckett Collection (color illustration, page 8)

Shika no ne no	The mountain
todokanu yama wa	no deer's cry has reached
mada aoshi	is still green

Otsuyu's poem resonates with a much earlier *waka* by the courtier Ōnakatomi no Yoshinobu (active circa 990):

Momiji senu	The deer who live
tokiwa no yama ni	without maple leaves
sumu shika o	on old pine mountain
onore nakite ya	can know that autumn has come
aki wo shiruran	only by their own cries

The difference between the two poems is instructive. In the *waka,* the scene is clearly spelled out. With no maple leaves turning red, the deer create their own sense of autumn. The haiku, on the other hand, suggests more than it defines. Could it be that the cries of the deer are not responses to autumn colors, but part of their cause? Botanists would object, but as expressions of feelings of loneliness and loss as the season changes, the cries of deer certainly evoke the interaction and interpenetration of nature, living creatures, and ourselves.

Otsuyu portrays the deer emerging from the mountain as if created from the same force of nature. Bending back towards the hills, the deer is composed of similar merging grey and black tones of ink, with horns and legs stretching diagonally up and down. The spidery calligraphy echoes the movements set up by the painting, creating a "U" shape for the total composition. Otsuyu's signature and seal form a closure to the calligraphy, just as the left leg of the deer anchors the painting. The painting, poem, and calligraphy all stress natural interconnection — this is the joy of haiga.

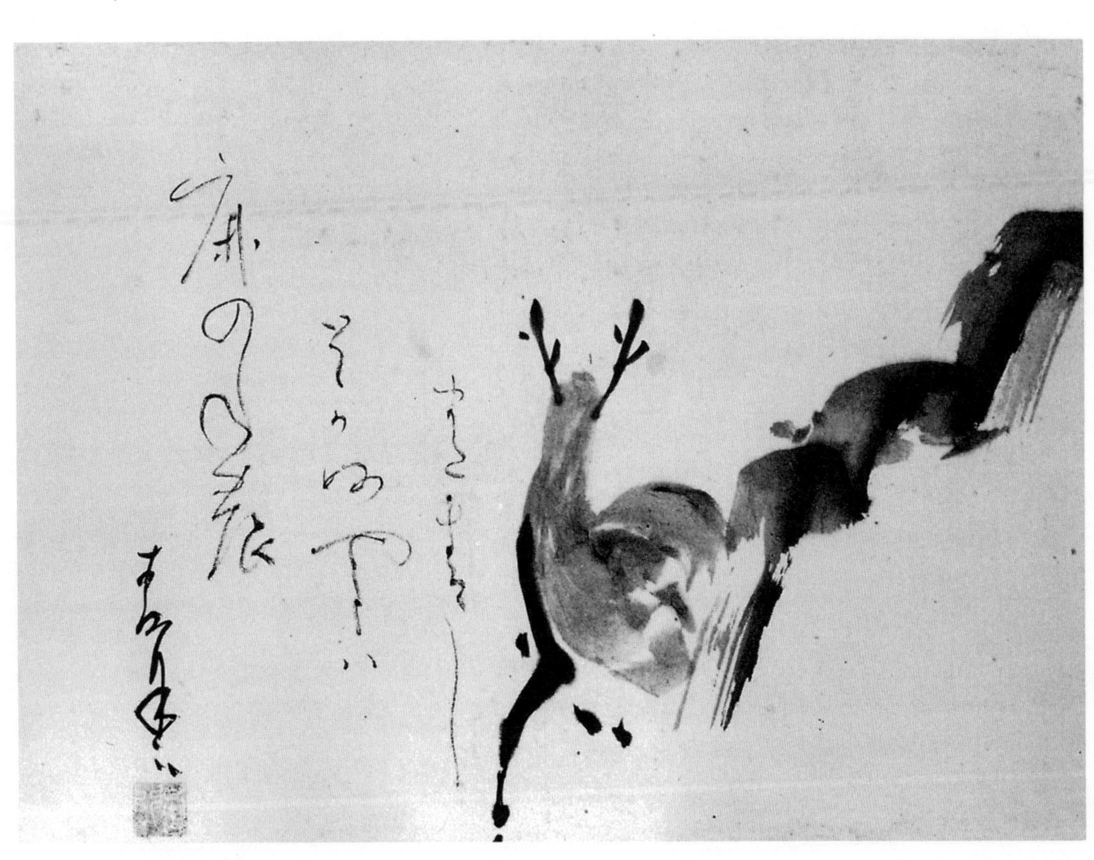

7. Kaga no Chiyo (1703-1775)

Late Spring

Ink on paper, 37 7/8 x 6 7/8 (96.3 x 17.7)
Yabumoto Collection, Tokyo

Chiyo, the daughter of a scroll-mounter, began composing haiku in her youth, so she was well prepared for creating and sometimes joining words and images. She studied with two of Bashō's leading pupils, Kagami Shikō (1665-1731) and Otsuyu, but when she was in her thirties, the deaths of her parents and older brother left her the responsibility of carrying on the family business. As she neared the age of fifty, Chiyo adopted a married couple and turned the scroll-mounting shop over to them. She then became a nun in 1754, and was once again able to devote much of her time and attention to haiku. Unlike most other women poets, she also became a master of haiga.

Boshun	*Late Spring*
Fuji no hana nagōte tsure ni okurekeri	As wisteria grows long, meeting companions is delayed

The poem creates a nice ambiguity — is the poet so fascinated with the flowers that she is late meeting her friends, or is she describing a tendril of wisteria that has not caught up with its fellows? Chiyo's composition is equally multilayered. The flowers fan out in the center of the composition, with calligraphy above and below. Tones of ink ranging from black to grey in the leaves contrast with the deeper black of the writing. The long trailing vine in the right center divides the final word of the poem, as though it were entwining both the poet and the blossoms in order to keep them from meeting their companions.

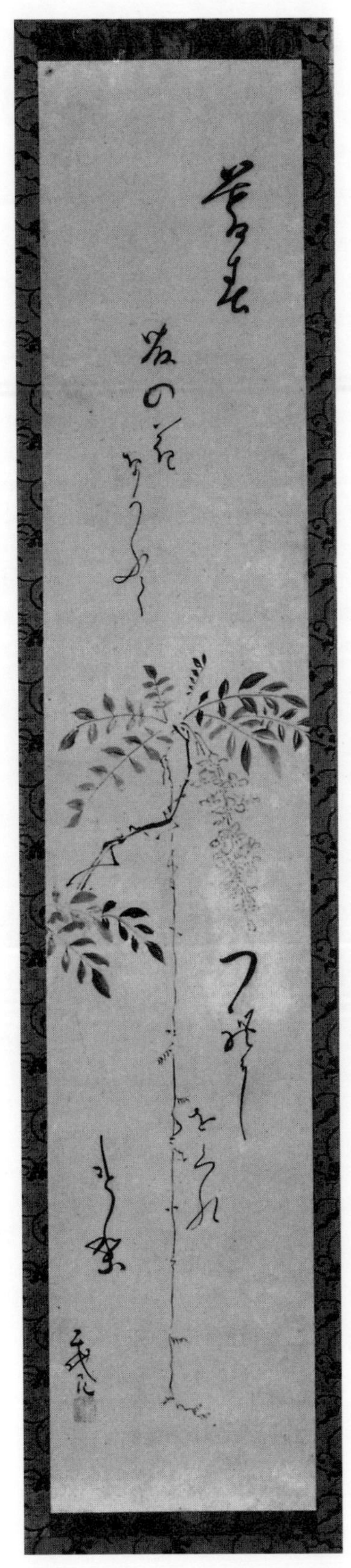

8. Yokoi Yayū (1702-1783)
Farming Ceremonies

Ink on paper, 38 1/8 x 11 3/8 (97 x 29)
Shinkeido Collection, Mesa, Arizona

Yayū represents the generation of poets who were beginning to move away from Bashō's influence towards greater humor and wit. He still revered the master, however, and maintained the primacy of personal experience in writing poetry. Born to a samurai family in Owari (Aichi Prefecture), Yayū served as a minister for the local *daimyō,* but also took up composing haiku, as had his grandfather and father before him. After some years of illness in his forties, he retired from his official position at the age of 52. Yayū devoted his final three decades to artistic pursuits, including poetry of many kinds, Noh drama, music, painting, and calligraphy. He became especially famous for mixtures of prose and poetry called *haibun* (haiku literature). His best-known work, *Uzuragoromo (Rags and Tatters),* was published after his death, and it is now considered one of the classics of Japanese literature.

In this scroll showing two Shinto priests, Yayū has created a rich intertwining of painting, prose, haiku, and *waka.* With a delicate touch in both painting and calligraphy, Yayū celebrates the spring and autumn farming festivals, begun in prehistoric Japan, which still exist today:

> When I visited the province of Harada, it was the time of the Shinto ritual for spring planting. The priests of the shrine were praying for the prosperity of the people while beating *tsutsumi* drums and chanting "Let's plant the seeds of good fortune!" The sight was holy and propitious. I drew a picture of the ceremonial hoe and gave this poem to the people:

Hata ni ta ni uchide no kuwa ya kozuchi yori	In fields and paddies the ceremonial hoe brings good fortune

> I again took an excursion to the village and stayed there from the beginning to the end of the eighth month. As the autumn was drawing near, I composed the following poem, celebrating the bountiful harvest:

Fukuwara no fukubuku to shite aki no ta no zen mo ho ni deyo sake mo ho ni deyo	New crops of good fortune radiantly sprouted in the autumn fields — Bring trays of food to the sheaves! Bring sake to the sheaves!

9. Miura Chora (1729-1780)

Descending Geese

Ink on paper, 35 5/8 x 19 7/8 (98.2 x 27.9)
Yabumoto Collection, Tokyo

Chora was born in Toba but lived most of his life in Ise Province, where he worked to bring the haiku tradition back to the simplicity and strength of Bashō. In 1772 he moved to Kyoto and became friends with haiku masters such as Buson. Chora enjoyed painting haiga in a free and simple style, such as these geese descending from the sky.

Hatsukari ya tsuki no soba yori arawaruru	Emerging from the regions of the moon — the first wild geese

The harbingers of autumn, wild geese had long been celebrated in Chinese and Japanese poetry and painting, but perhaps never before so simply. Here the painting suggests a haiku by the earlier master Shintoku (1633-1698):

Bonno kubo ni kari ochikakaku shimoyo kana	Wild geese falling right down my neck — frosty night

Chora's geese descend from the upper right of the composition, leaving a great deal of space in which they, the calligraphy, and perhaps our own imaginations, can fly.

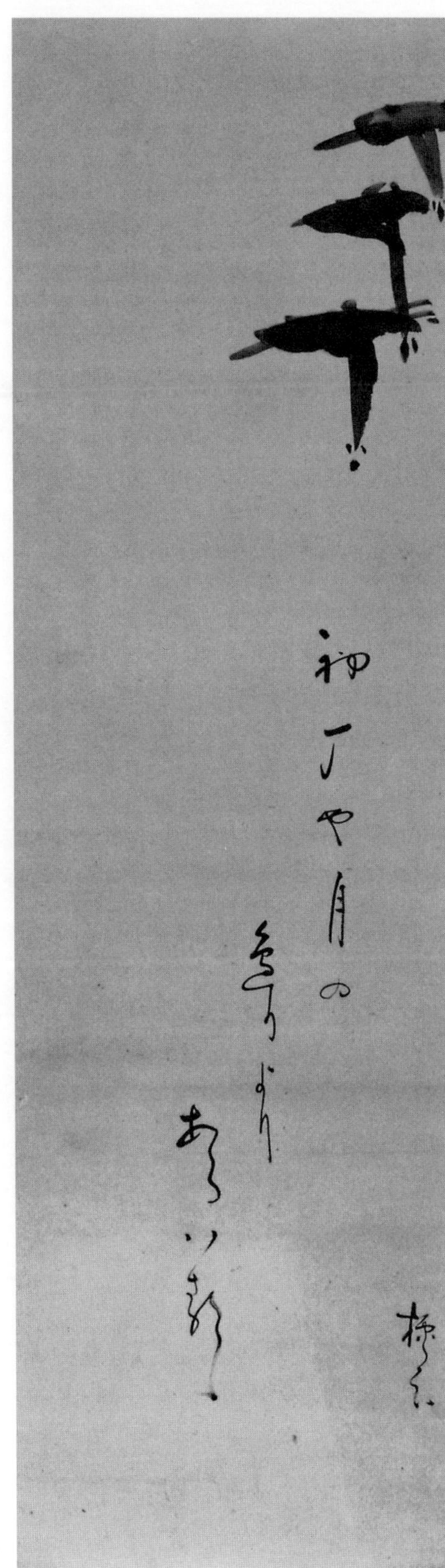

10. Takebe Ayatari, also known as Ryōtai (1719-1794)
Moon

Ink on paper, 12 x 19 1/8 (30.5 x 48.6)
Shōka Collection

Takebe Ayatari, whose name as a painter was Ryōtai, became one of the most versatile poet-artists of the early modern period. Born to a samurai family in northern Japan, he left home at the age of twenty, reportedly because of a scandalous affair with the wife of his older brother. Forced to fend for himself, he spent his life devoted to the arts. Through the research of the scholar Lawrence Marceau, Ayatari emerges as a fascinating personality, with a range of interests and abilities that made him an extremely significant figure in the world of poetry and art in the second half of the eighteenth century.

Ayatari became known as a leading haiku poet in Edo, but instead of pursuing a comfortable career writing and teaching, he decided to learn Chinese-style literati painting. Since Chinese were restricted to the port city of Nagasaki, Ayatari traveled there twice, studying first with a Japanese expert and later with the visiting Chinese merchant-artist Fei Han-yuan. Ayatari was one of the very few Japanese painters to study directly with a Chinese artist, and in order to spread the understanding of literati brushwork, he published a number of woodblock books of both Chinese works and his own paintings. Although Ayatari almost went blind at one point in his career, he continued to paint, and most of his extant works are landscapes and other subjects in Chinese style. However, as a leading haiku poet, Ayatari also created haiga that are quite different from his usual, much more complex literati brushwork.

In this work from his middle years, Ayatari has taken the concept of a simplified image to its ultimate, a single line. This relaxed, curving brushstroke in varied grey inktones creates a moon in one corner of the composition, while the bold and slightly meandering calligraphy of his poem fills the rest of the space:

Yoru naraba	In the evening
abunaki hashi ya	the bridge becomes dangerous —
kyō no tsuki	tonight's moon

Ayatari leaves us with the question: exactly why does the bridge become dangerous?

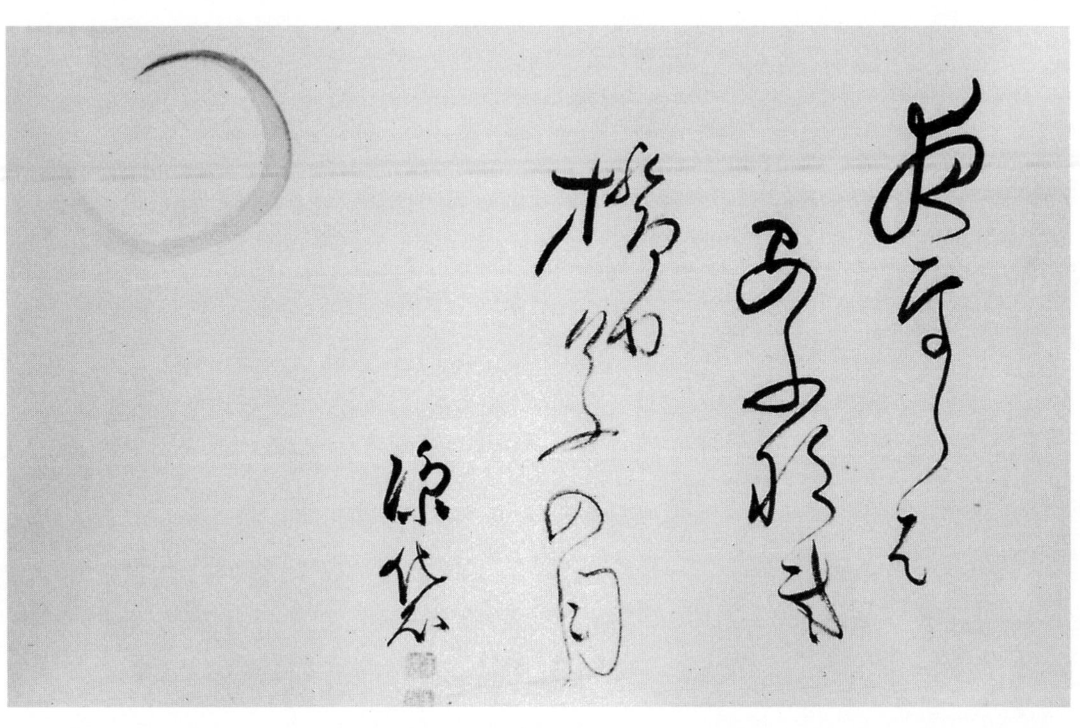

11. Yosa Buson (1716-1784)
Portrait of Chigetsu, 1799

Woodblock book print, 10 1/2 x 7 7/8 (26.8 x 19.3)
Private Collection

Buson was the second great master of haiku, in part by insisting upon Bashō's primacy during an age when haiku was moving away from the direct expression of experience that Bashō had fostered. Buson solidified his own position in what he considered the true succession by painting several versions of Bashō's travel journeys as well as portraits of the master. In addition, Buson honored other haiku poets of previous decades by painting an album that was later used as the model for the woodblock book *Haikai sanjūrokkasen (Thirty-six Haiku Masters).* First printed in 1799, it includes this portrait of the poet Chigetsu. Buson's images in this album were patterned upon the "Thirty-Six Immortal Poets" of *waka,* who had been anthologized and depicted many times over the previous centuries. Buson's portraits, however, are much more relaxed and informal than those of the *waka* tradition.

For the poet Chigetsu (1632-1706), a pupil of Bashō who became a nun, Buson integrated the calligraphy of one of her haiku poems with the curving outlines of her face and robe:

Toshiyoreba	When it grows old
koe mo kanashiki	its voice becomes plaintive —
kirigirisu	katydid

Chigetsu looks down, as though listening to the weakening call of the insect as summer ends. Even in this woodblock print, Buson's fluent skill as a painter is apparent. Indeed, he became one of the great masters of the literati school of painters in the Chinese tradition. Yet he also painted haiga until the end of his life, and it was the haiku spirit of warmth, intuition, suggestion, and human interaction with nature that characterized his painting even when he worked in a more elaborate Chinese-derived style.

The additional painterly skill that Buson brought to haiga led to a new mini-tradition in which his haiga, and those of his followers Goshun, Baitei, and Kinkoku, have been highly admired by art lovers, including those with no particular interest in haiku poetry. This may have been one more reason why Buson painted portraits of his predecessors; he was establishing his roots as a Japanese poet-painter, rather than only a professional artist.

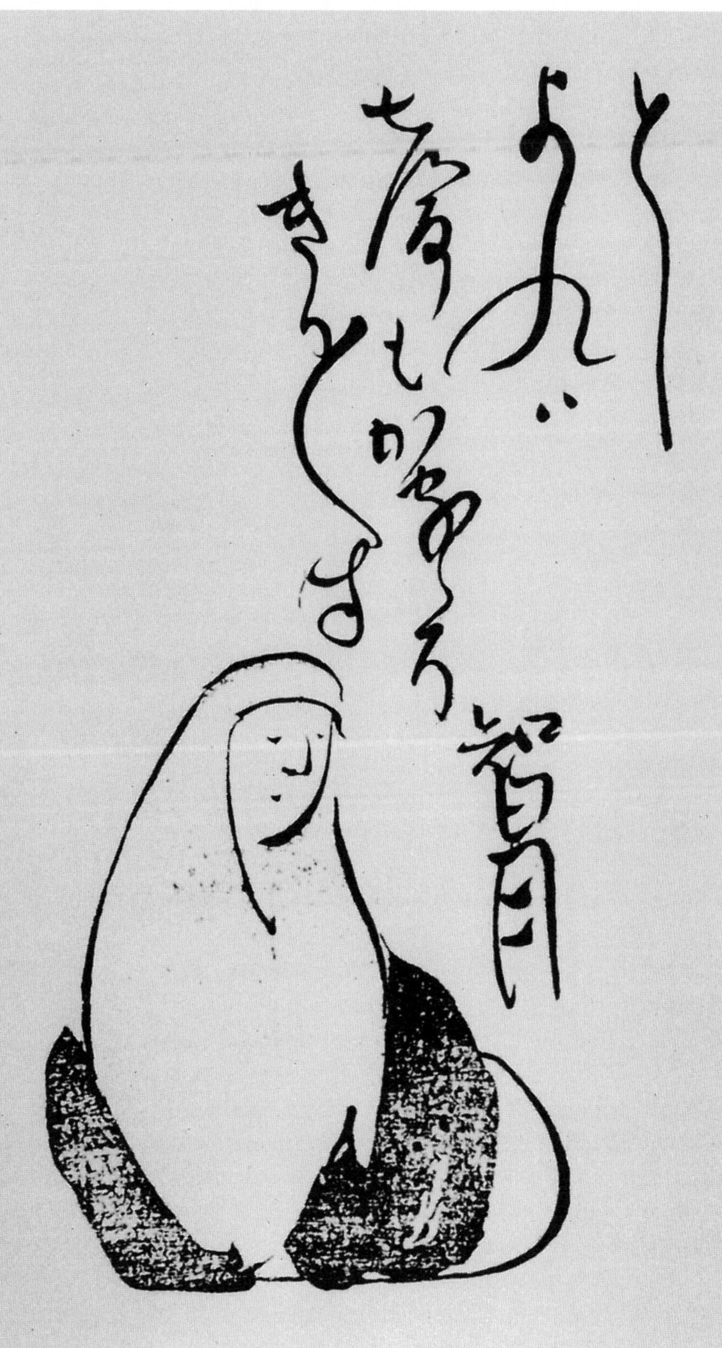

12. Yosa Buson (1716-1784)

Rocks Fan

Ink on paper, 5 3/4 x 18 1/2 (17.1 x 47)
Sanso Collection, United States

Buson often painted rocks, sometimes allowing them to float freely over the surface of the painting with no anchor to the realities of ground and gravity. Despite the simplicity of the subject, it carries with it allusions to Chinese and Japanese poets of the past. The scholars Calvin French, Okada Rihei, Aoki Masaru, and John Rosenfield have all studied Buson's rock paintings and followed his multiple allusions to their sources.

First, the Chinese poet Su Shih (1037-1101) made two journeys to the Red Cliff, where a great battle had been fought centuries earlier. He wrote two famous prose poems that express the constant change in human affairs amid the ultimate changelessness of nature as represented by moon and river. During his second visit, Su Shih found the river running low, with "rocks jutting forth here and there."

Second, the Japanese wandering monk-poet Saigyō (1118-1190) wrote a *waka* about the "wanderer's willow" of Ashino village:

Michi no be ni	Along the road
shimizu nagaruru	a pure stream flows
yanagi kage	in the shade of a willow
shibashi to te koso	wanting to rest
tachidomaritsure	I paused — and have not left

Third, Bashō visited this "wanderer's willow" in 1669, and recalling Saigyō, wrote the haiku:

Ta ichimai	One rice field planted
uete tachisaru	before I would leave —
yanagi kana	the willow

When Buson visited the same willow in 1743, he composed the haiku on this painting:

Yanagi chiri	Willow bare
shimizu kare	clear stream dried up
ishi tokoro-dokoro	rocks here and there

But why is the willow now bare and the stream dried up? Did Buson feel that the great East Asian poetry tradition from Su Shih and Saigyō to Bashō had become bare and dry in his day? In his other writings it is clear that Buson was unhappy with directions taken in haiku during the post-Bashō era, when clever wordplay gradually became more important than the extraordinary perception of ordinary experience. For Buson, it was important to take his place among the great poets of the past, and this could only be done by following their lead in personal expression. Poetically for Buson there was no shade from the willow, no clear stream, only rocks. And that's what he painted.

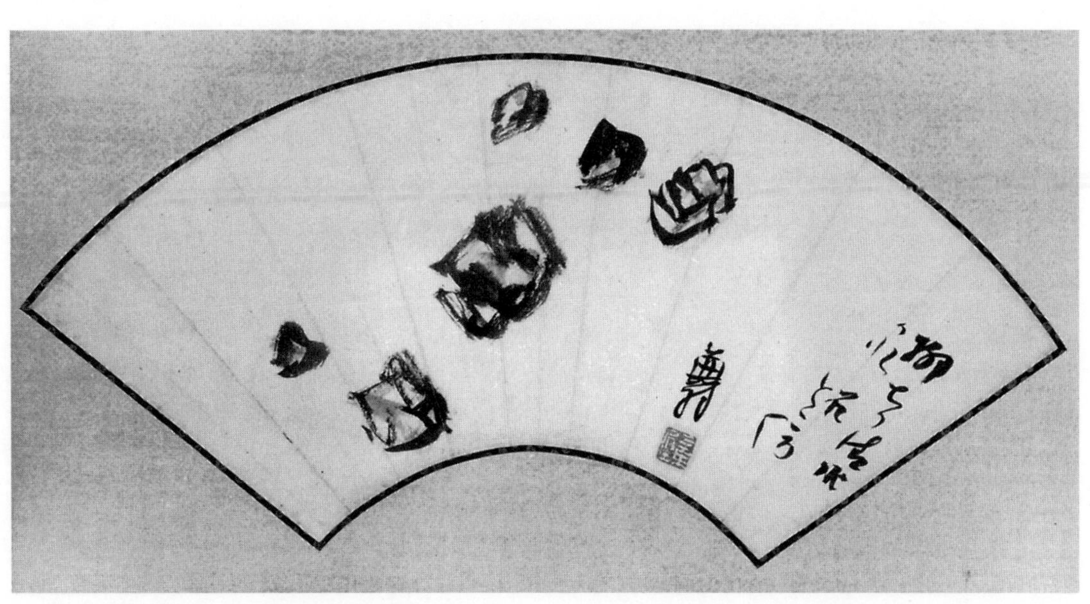

13. Matsumura Goshun (1752-1811)

Age Fifty

Ink and light color on paper, 7 x 6 1/2 (18 x 16.7)
Private Collection (color illustration, page 6)

Goshun was Buson's closest disciple in painting, and also followed his master in creating haiga with smooth and relaxed brushwork. Here a man dressed in formal New Year's clothing sits facing a haiku poem, with a curving band of negative space between the image and the calligraphy. The closed fan creates a diagonal accent at the bottom center, reinforcing the line of the man's folded leg and pointing to the haiku.

Gojū kara	Because you're fifty
kazoe yo chiyo no	count the New Year's pine branches
matsukazari	of a thousand ages

In traditional Japan, people were considered one year older on New Year's Day, which therefore became everyone's birthday. The age of fifty was special because it was considered the beginning of respected old age. Therefore the boughs of the evergreen pine, a traditional New Year's decoration, also carry here the meaning of long life. In addition, the tall forehead on the figure suggests the extended head of Jurōjin, the god of good fortune who also represents longevity. Finally, on the back of the figure is the auspicious Buddhist jewel symbol. So for a man reaching the age of fifty, everything about this small painting is celebratory: Happy Birthday, Happy New Year, and Long Life!

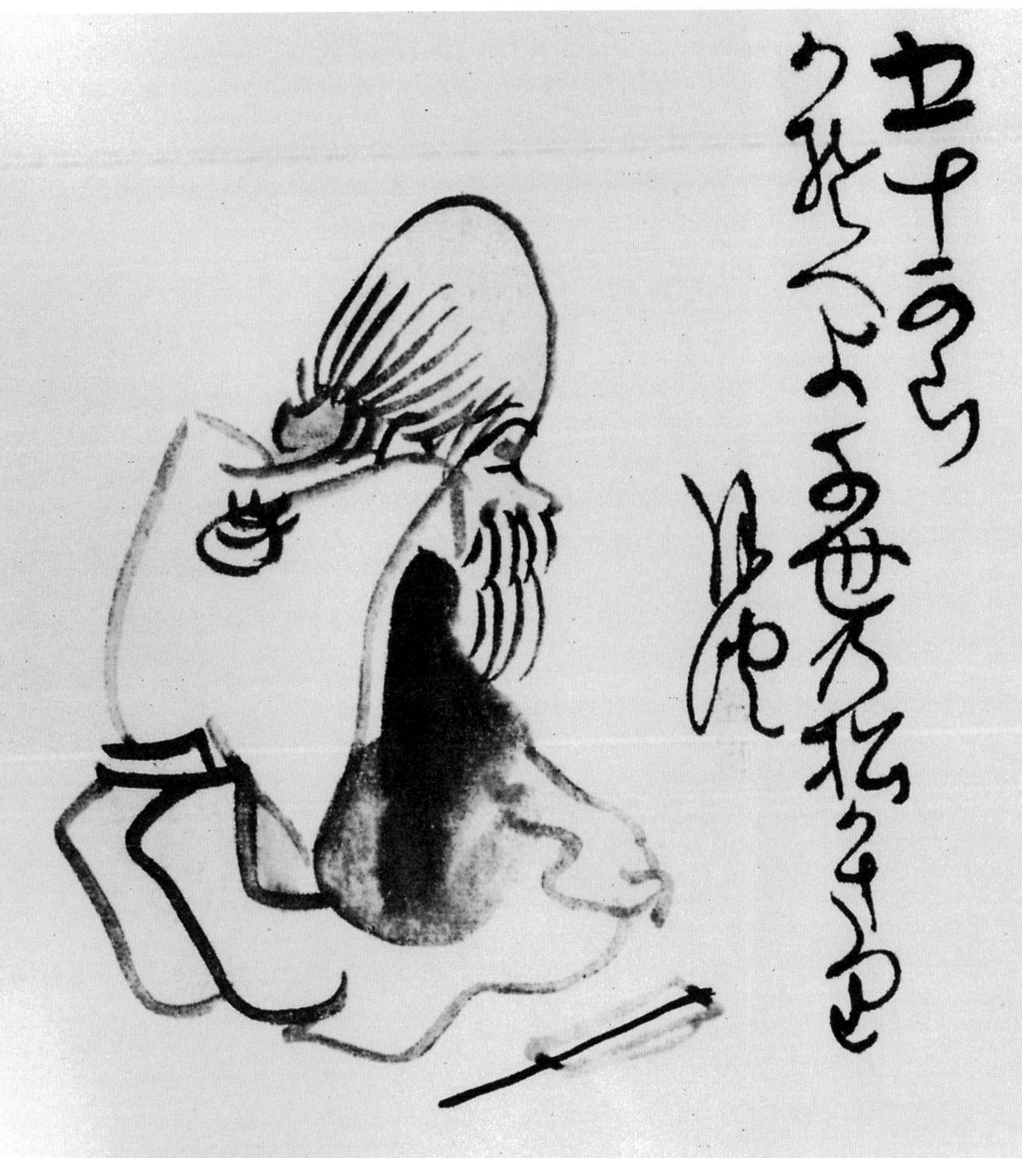

14. Ki Baitei (1734-1810)

Portrait of Bashō

Ink on paper, 11 3/4 x 10 1/2 (30 x 26.8)
Private Collection

The high regard that Buson held for Bashō was also felt by Buson's pupil Baitei, who portrayed the master several times in various sizes and formats. Here, in a small painting that may have originally served as an album leaf, Baitei shows Bashō seated facing the viewer with his hat and traveling box, ready for a poetic journey.

Baitei depicted Bashō in relaxed outlines and tones of grey, but he gave equal space to writing out a pair of introductions about and poems by Bashō, referring to trips the master took without his haiku friend Etsujin:

This time, they say he didn't take Etsujin along:

Samukeredo	Even when it's cold
futari tabine wa	it's more interesting to travel
omoshirōki	together

Intending to send it to Etsujin, the next year he composed this poem:

Futari mishi	The snow we saw together —
yuki wa kotoshi mo	does it fall
furikeru ka	this year as well?

The two poems about friendship both contain the word *futari,* literally meaning "two people" but here signifying "together" or "the two of us." But Baitei has only pictured the single figure of Bashō. Who is the second person in this haiga, the friend of the poet? Certainly it might be Baitei, who honored Bashō with this portrait. But couldn't it also be any one of us?

此度ハ越人と [illegible]
[illegible]
[illegible]二人旅寝せし
おもしろさ
[illegible]越人の方へつかハしたるとて
二人見し雪ハ[illegible]降けるか
はせを [illegible]

15. Ki Baitei (1734-1810)

Calligraphy by Kōnan Setsuko (n.d.)

Thirty Figures

Ink and color on paper; two panels, each 68 1/4 x 35 1/2 (173.4 x 89.7)
Shōka Collection (left panel: color illustration, page 13)

Although Baitei was one of Buson's closest followers, he excelled in painting rather than haiku, and so his haiga usually are inscribed with poems by Buson and other poets. In this case Setsuko, probably a literary friend of Baitei from his home area of Lake Biwa, inscribed the screens with poems that were almost always composed by the figures portrayed. Strangely, while the left screen shows only haiku poets, the right screen includes other figures; in these cases three lines from their *waka* or *renga* were chosen, or a haiku poem about them was added.

These screens were first published in the 1974 exhibition catalogue by Calvin French and his students entitled *The Poet-Painters: Buson and His Followers.* The numerical chart is taken from that publication, which offers translations of all the poems. Here we can concentrate upon a few of the most interesting figures and associated verses. In these screens, Baitei was clearly placing the haiku tradition within the larger scope of Japanese history and poetry, and we can follow the continuous stream of Japanese poets by excerpting some major figures:

Poet #12 is the courtier, man of letters and *waka* master Fujiwara Teika (1162-1241), with one of his sections from a *renga:*

Chiru hana o oikakete yuku arashi kana	Fallen blossoms — the stormy wind in swift pursuit

Poet #4 is the Zen Master Ikkyū Sōjun (1394-1481); his poem is taken from a *renga* about the Gion park in Kyoto:

Dengaku no amami ni masaru kyō no tsuki	Excelling the sweetness of bean cakes — tonight's moon

Poet #9 is Arakida Moritake (1473-1549), one of the first masters of haiku:

Ganchō ya kamiyo no koto mo omowaruru	New Year's Day — my thoughts return to the deities

Poet #19 is Bashō (1644-1694); the dedicatory haiku by Hōga Isshō (1643-1707) utilizes the literal meaning of the name Bashō as "banana plant."

Fune to nari ho to naru kaze no bashō kana	Become a boat, become a sail — wind in the banana plants

Poet #2 is Bashō's pupil Chigetsu (1632-1706), looking rather more elegant than in the portrait by Buson:

Wazato sae mi ni yuku tabi o Fuji no yuki	Only one reason for going sightseeing — snow on Mount Fuji

Poet #16, who repeats as poet #23, is Uejima Onitsura (1661-1738), a masseur who became a monk:

Gyōzui no sutedokoro naki mushi no koe	No place to throw the dirty bath water — insect voices

Poet #8 is Chiyo (1703-1775), and her poem is said to have been written the day after her marriage:

Shibukaro ka shiranedo kaki no hatsu chigiri	Bitter or sweet? the first picking of the persimmon

Baitei does not include his teacher Buson, but one unusual figure in his painting is a sumo wrestler (#28) with a haiku by Aida Gozan (1717-1787):

Hito tsukami iza mairasen toshi no kure	Let's practice one more time — the end of the year

Note: the other figures on the right screen are #1 Karasumaru Mitsuhiro (1579-1638), #2 Kyūraku (n.d.), #3 Minamoto Yoshiie (1038-1108), #5 Sanjōnishi Sanetaka (n.d.), #6 Minamoto Yoritomo (1147-1199), #7 Ninagawa Chikamasa (d. 1652), #9 Arakida Moritake (1473-1549), #10 Hatakeyama Shigetada (1164-1205), #11 Shōkadō Shōjō (1584-1639), #13 unknown poetess, and #14 Saitō Tokugen (1559-1647) who is also #24 on the left screen.

Continuing on the left screen are #15 Tateba Fukaku (1661-1752), #17 Ōdaka Shiyō (1660-1693), #18 Sakuden (n.d.), #20 Sugiki Mitsujo (1583-1647), #21 Hattori Ransetsu (1654-1707), #25 Yasuhara Teishitsu 1609-1673), #26 Katsuyama (n.d.), #27 Hirose Izen (1646-1711), #29 Mukai Kyorai (1651-1704), and #30 Enomoto Kikaku (1661-1707).

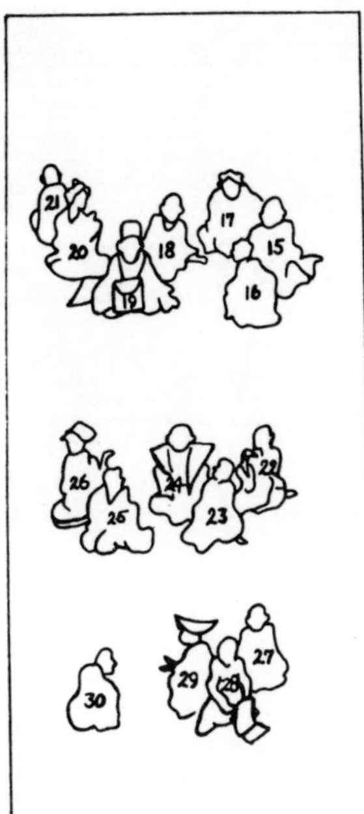

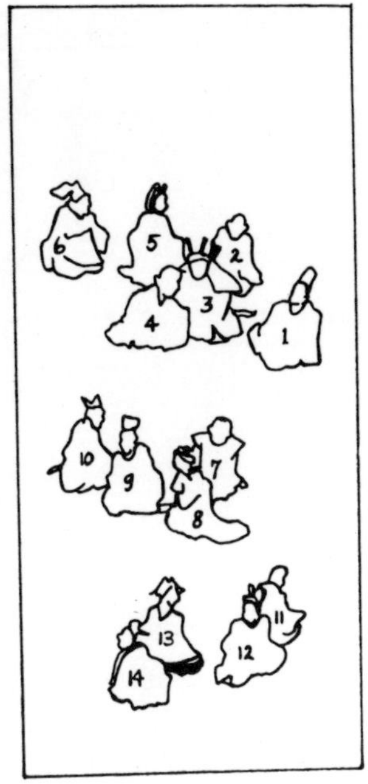

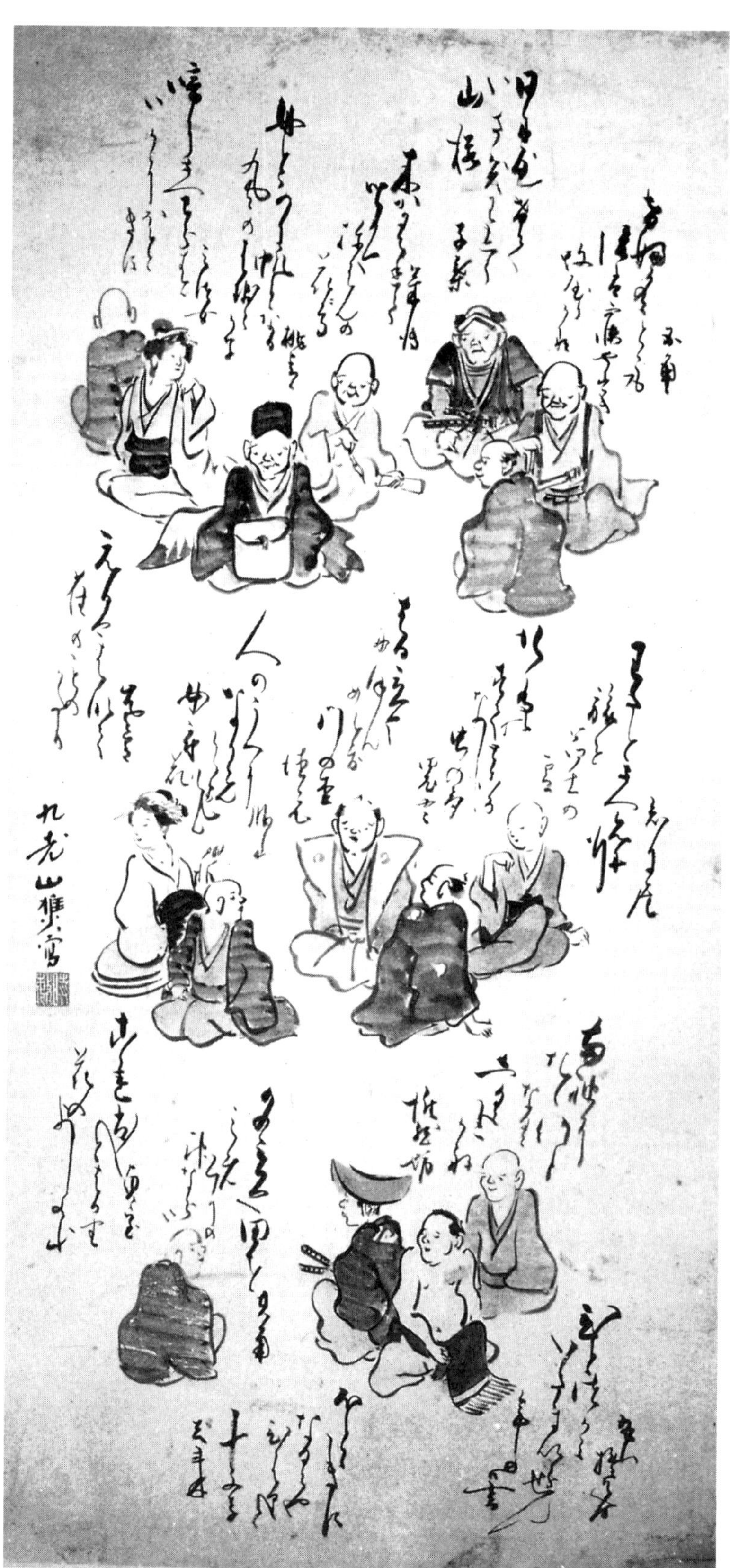

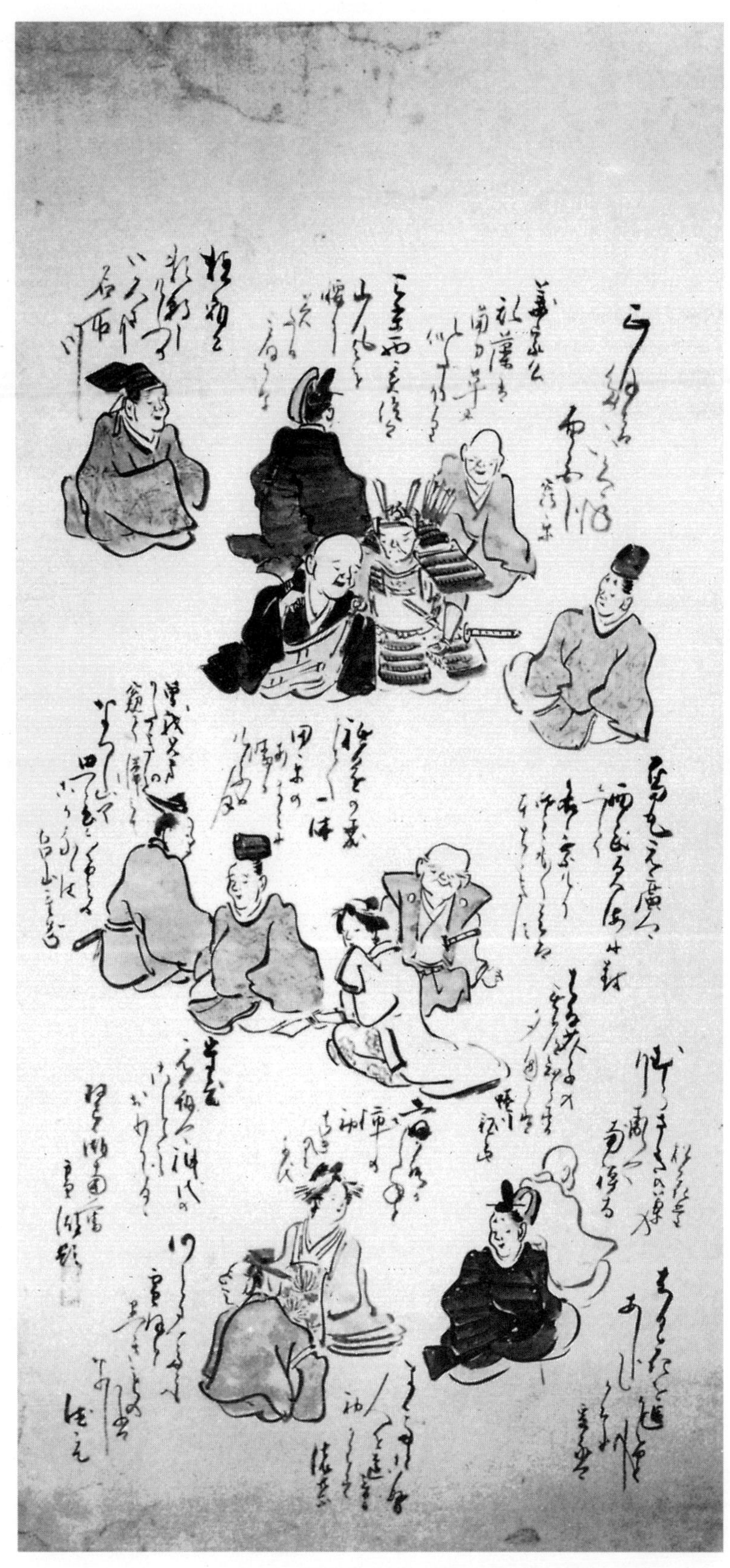

16. Yokoi Kinkoku (1761-1832

Sora Parting from Bashō

Ink and light color on paper, 26 3/4 x 11 (68 x 28)
Beckett Collection

Kinkoku had an interesting career as a monk, painter, and adventurer. He spent most of his life in Shiga Prefecture, where he practiced the esoteric rituals of Buddhist mountain monks, and thereupon sold his landscape paintings as charms. He also lived for a time in Nagoya, where he befriended haiku poets such as Inoue Shirō (Cat. Nos. 35-37). In painting, Kinkoku followed Buson to the point that it is sometimes erroneously thought that he was Buson's direct pupil. Instead, Kinkoku followed Buson's style, sometimes copying his paintings with personal and often impetuous brushwork. Here is one of Kinkoku's most restrained scrolls, a sensitive image of the poet Sora parting from his master Bashō during his famous journey to the "interior" Northern provinces.

Buson, in order to honor Bashō (and also to establish himself as Bashō's true follower), had several times copied and illustrated Bashō's *Narrow Road to the Interior* in handscroll and screen formats. Kinkoku has here followed Buson's style to depict the moment when Sora must leave his master "like paired geese parting in the skies." However, Kinkoku has used the format of a hanging scroll rather than a handscroll or screen, giving more space to the figures. In addition, the taller format allowed Kinkoku the unique idea of stamping Bashō's seals rather than adding a poetic inscription, making this work a haiku-related painting rather than a formal haiga. The top seal appears to have been one that Bashō himself used on many of his works. This combination of painting and seals is an unusual homage to the master, and serves as Kinkoku's artistic bow to the serene figure of Japan's greatest haiku poet.

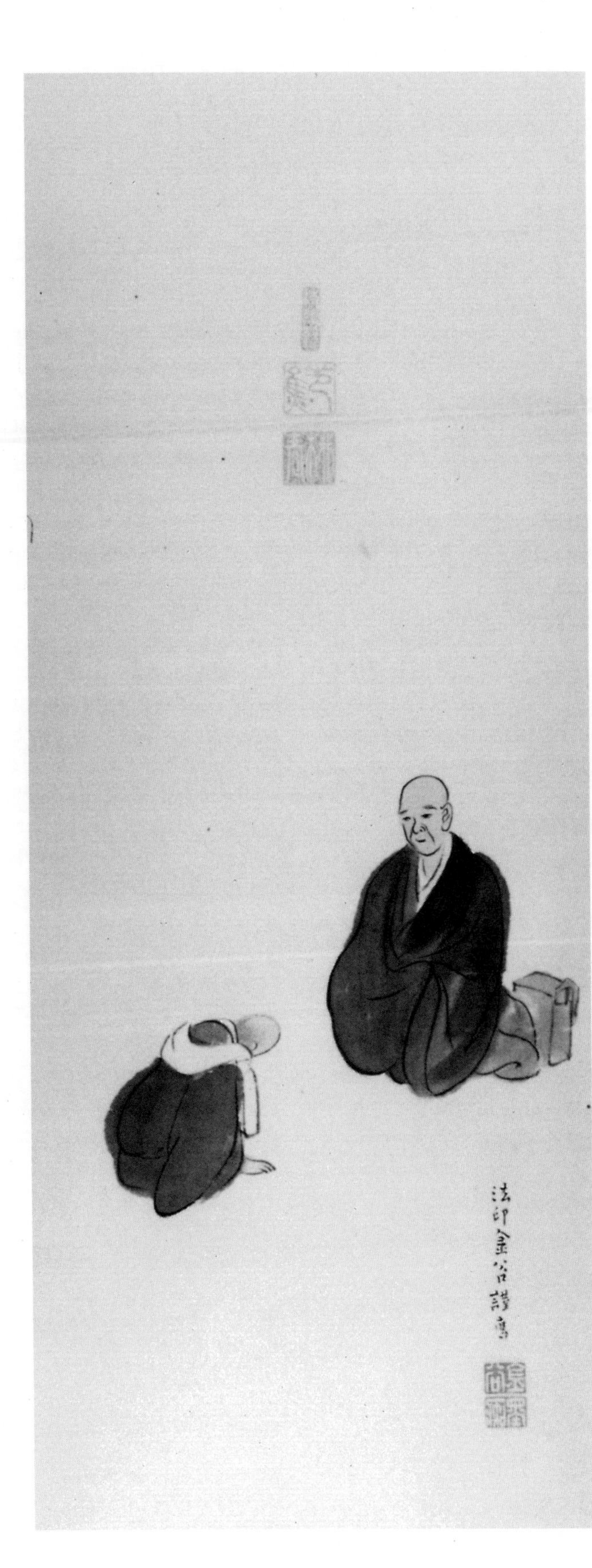
法印金谷謹寫

17. Yamaguchi Soken (1759-1818)
Inscription by Takahashi Senan (?-1831)
Crow and Persimmons

Ink and color on paper, 49 x 11 (124.5 x 27.9)
Man'yo-an Collection, New Orleans

Yamaguchi Soken was one of the major pupils of the naturalistic master Maruyama Ōkyo (1733-1795), who had created a new style from a blending of Western, Chinese, and Japanese traditions. Emphasizing the direct study from nature, Ōkyo founded the Maruyama school of painting which was to achieve great success in Kyoto and Osaka. Soken's own specialty was the detailed and evocative painting of beautiful women, but he also had a great range as an artist, depicting birds and flowers, animals, landscapes, and scenes of everyday life in Kyoto.

Here Soken paints a moment of late autumn: a crow is examining two persimmons on a drooping branch. Soken spaces his composition masterfully: the diagonal of the crow's body contrasts with the curving branch, while his twisting head provides a counter-accent that helps to unify the four main compositional areas within the tall narrow format of the scroll.

Soken's brushwork shows the influence of Goshun, who midway through his career left Buson's literati artistic tradition and joined Ōkyo in pursuing more naturalistic styles of painting. During this later stage of his career, Goshun often painted with a flat brush, creating "washes" of ink and color that show gradations of tones within a single brushstroke. Soken has utilized this flat brush technique to depict the crow, the persimmons, and the leaves; there is no need for calligraphic brushwork, or even specific outlines. Instead, Soken renders an impressionistic view of the bird eyeing the fruits as though counting their numbers and discerning their ripeness.

Senan was a pupil of the poet Kaya Shirao (1738-1791) from Nagano. His haiku, translated by Kinuko Jambor, brings forth another aspect of the autumn season:

Meigetsu ya	The full moon!
namida soete wa	my tears are not enough
hometarazu	to praise it

Aside from their seasonal connection, the interactions between the painting and the verse are subtle. They both suggest viewing; while people may enjoy the moon, the crow seems more interested in the fruit. As for the tears, might they be visually suggested by the shapes of the persimmons and leaves? And if so, are there enough persimmons for the birds to praise?

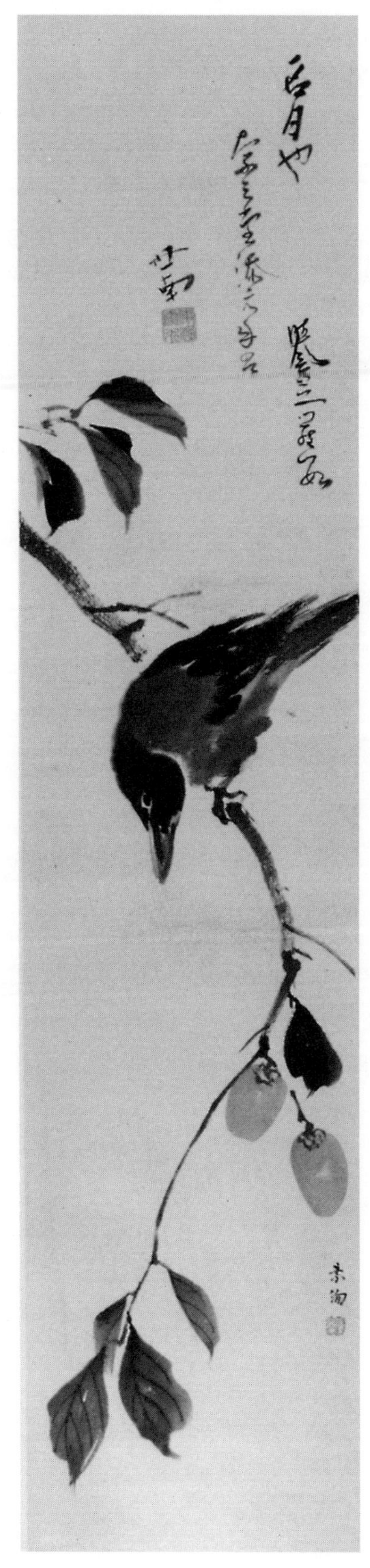

18. Takebe Sōchō (1761-1814)
Screens of the Twelve Months

Ink and color on paper; two six-panel screens, each 62 5/8 x 136 (59 x 348)
Masuda Shōzaburō Collection, Tokyo (detail: color illustration, frontispiece)

Haiga screens are very rare, mostly because the combination of haiku and image is usually best created in modest formats and sizes. However, Sōchō produced a tour-de-force by combining twelve individual panels into six pairs of paintings on two screens, representing the twelve months with prose introductions, haiku, and paintings. Moving leftwards from the right panel of the right screen, we can follow the activities of a full year.

First month, a broom and a New Year's decoration:

When I traveled through the countryside of Harima, I stayed at Takasago Bay. Here in the home of a man named Fushu I saw a calligraphy by my late father Ryūsai; there is a deep connection between the two generations. At the New Year, I still remained in Naniwa.

Takasago ni
oya no sho mo ari
fude hajime

At Takasago
my father's calligraphy —
first brushwork of the year

Second month, the courtier-poet Ariwara Narihira and an attendant:

The place where I live is called Sekiya Village, only one hundred steps from the Sumida River. It is a beautiful area, famous for the moon and snow:

Asa no ma ni
sakura mite kite
oinikeri

Through the morning
I watched cherry blossoms
become old

Shirauo no
kokora de haramu
sakura kana

Here is where
whitefish spawn —
cherry blossoms

Getauri ya
hatsuharu goto ni
koume mura

Clogs-seller —
every year as spring begins
at small plum village

Third month, a cuckoo:

To someone who reads the *Tsurezuregusa [Essays in Idleness* by Yoshida Kenkō]:

Higashiyama
totte kaese ya
hototogisu

Hurry back
to Higashiyama —
cuckoo

Fourth month, a crescent moon:

The dyeing of cloth in Edo is better than in other areas, excelling not only Shiraki-ya, but also Echigo-ya [the names of stores].

Hototogisu
kutan kaketa yo
Murasaki-ya

The cuckoo
calls "Nine Bolts Displayed"
Murasaki-ya

Fifth month, a man pulling a horse:

On a journey, the Festival of Tango:

Uma karite
Ikaho ni asoban
Ayame kana

Let's rent a horse
and enjoy at Ikaho —
irises

Yūgao ya
ware ga io ni
samo nitari

Evening glories
just like those
at our hermitage

Sixth month, a traveler questioning a farming woman:

Susuki kara
ka no deru yado ni
tomarikeri

From pampas grasses
mosquitoes came into the inn
where I stayed

Iroiro no
shimizu o musubu
Yamaji kana

Various clear streams
all tied together —
mountain path

Nemu saku ya
tsuge no kokushi mo
hoshige ni te

Seeming to desire
a small boxwood comb —
the blooming silktree

Seventh Month, a lute:

The seventh day of the seventh month:

Matsushima ya
sareba koto hiku
aki no kaze

Matsushima
and yet a koto sounds —
autumn wind

Country house:

Otozururu mo
tou mo samushi
tsuki hitoyo

Both the visitor
and the questioner are cold
one moonlit night

Uchitsuke ni
shimizu no sato ya
kyō no tsuki

Just as it is
the village of clear waters —
tonight's moon

Eighth month, morning glories and a mouth-organ made from bamboo tubes:

When facing an inkstone, one wants to write, and when taking up a instrument, one wants to create music [a quote from the *Tsurezuregusa]:*

Ro ni yoreba
kamo ga matarete
kamo no koe

Leaning on the hearth
and waiting for the duck to roast —
the call of wild geese

At the house of a samurai:

Asagao ya
kesa wa izure ni
mato kaken

Morning glories —
this morning, where can I
hang my target?

Ninth month, the thunder god:

A story while traveling in Sōchū:

Ashigara wa
mada denu kami no
todoro kana

At Ashigara —
the roar of the god
has not yet emerged

Tenth month, a landscape painting:

Tokikaze de
hama wa fukunari
kure no kaze

Seasonal winds
blow at the beach —
darkening winds

Yuku kari no
ato o nigiwasu
Ashiya kana

After the departing
geese, the merry-making —
Ashiya

Eleventh month, a puppeteer:

Returning from Tennō-ji:

Tatsurō ga
taiko kikoyuru
kareno kana

Listening to
Tatsurō's drum —
withered fields

Keisei wa
mino mo tashiname
hatsu shigure

The courtesan
scolds even the straw coat —
first winter rain

Chikuma River:

Echigo kara
futatsu tsurete ya
ukinegamo

They've come as a pair
from Echigo —
floating ducks

Twelfth month, a man dancing with his hat:

Coming to Ikuta forest, where winter cherry trees are planted by the side of the beach. Since this is a shrine with ancient ceremonies:

Koyuki seyo
kasa kite mawan
kami no mae

Let the light snow fall
I'll dance with my sedge hat
in front of the god

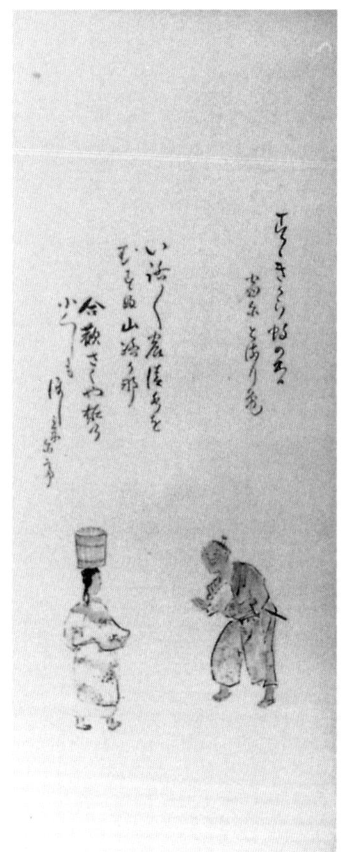

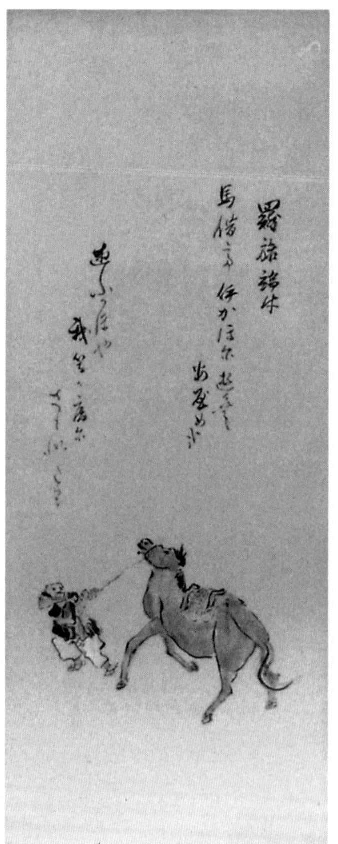

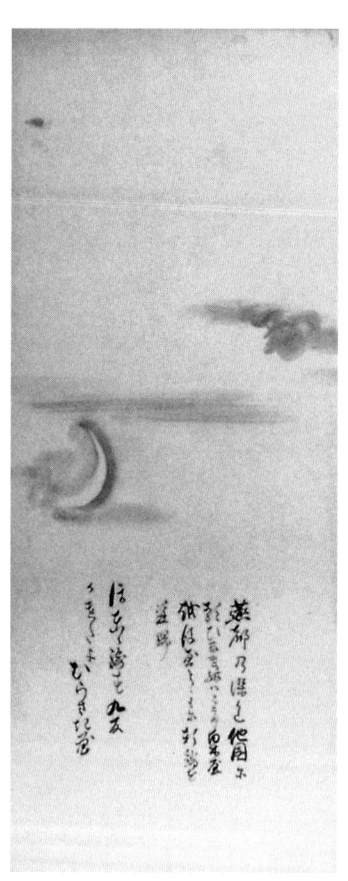

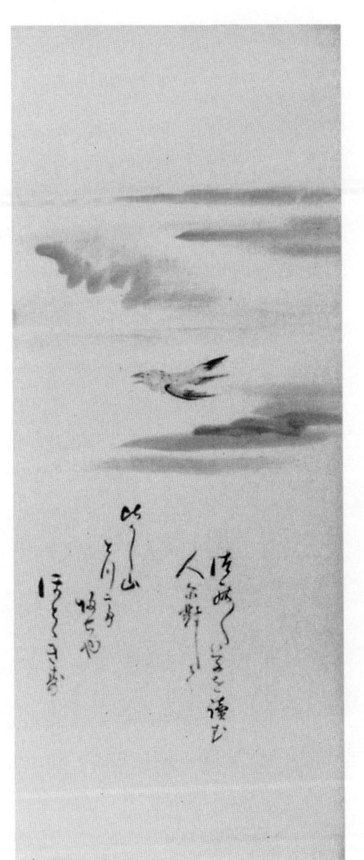

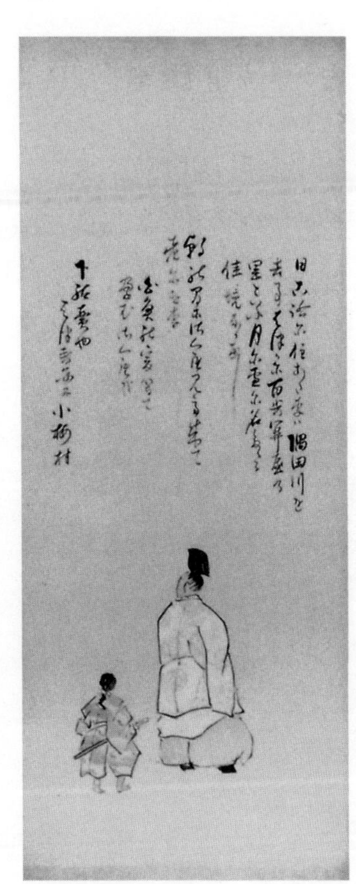

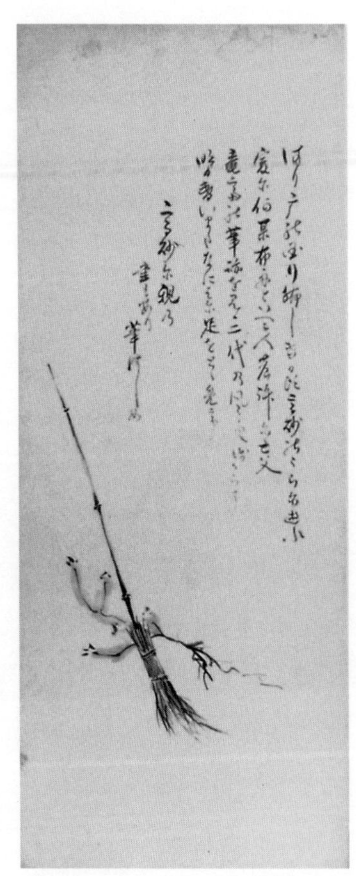

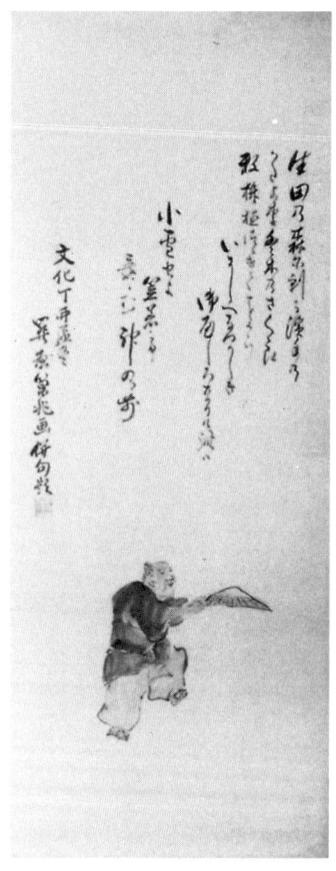

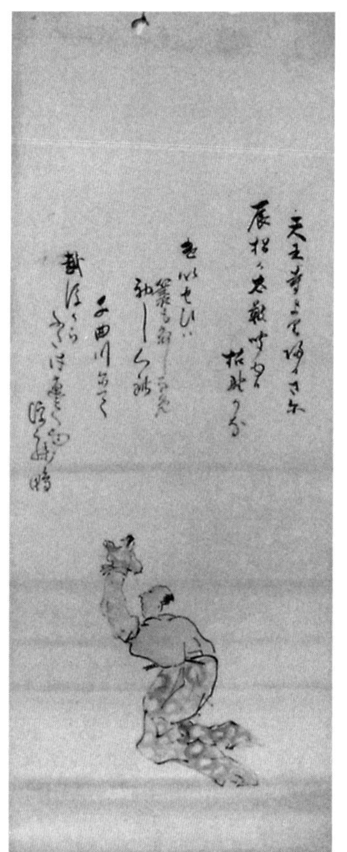

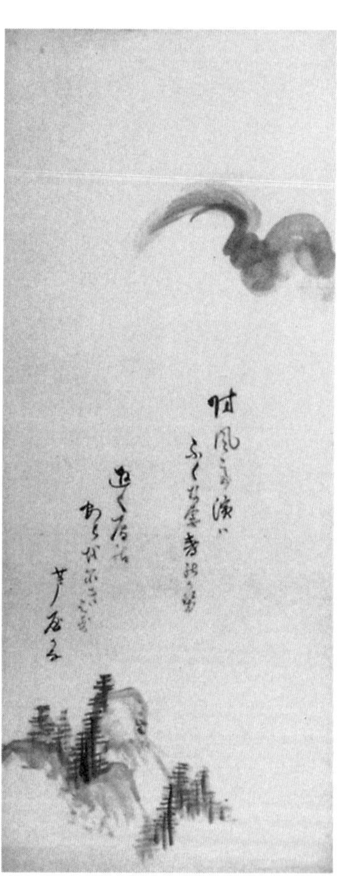

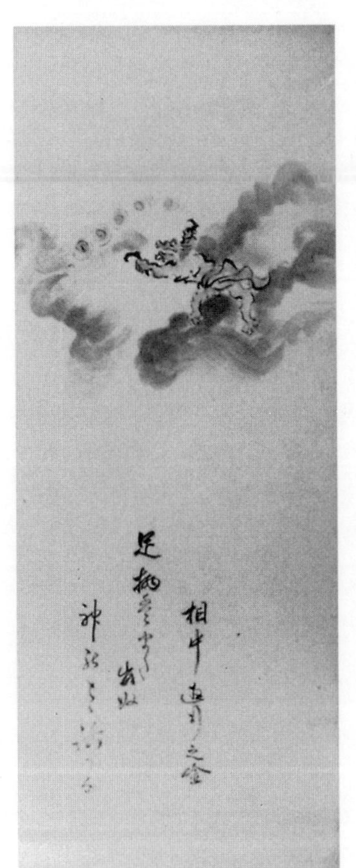

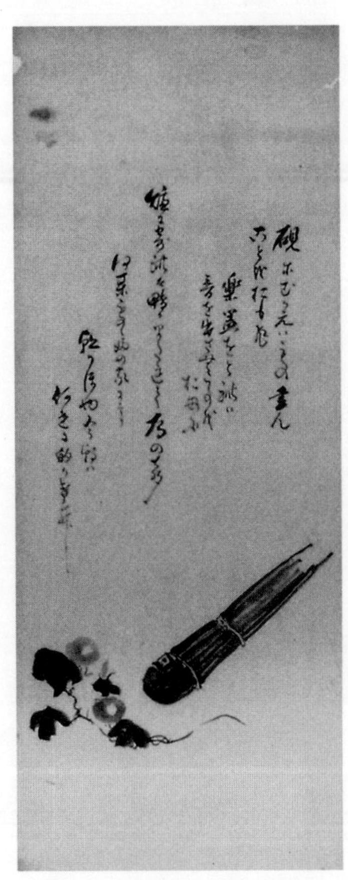

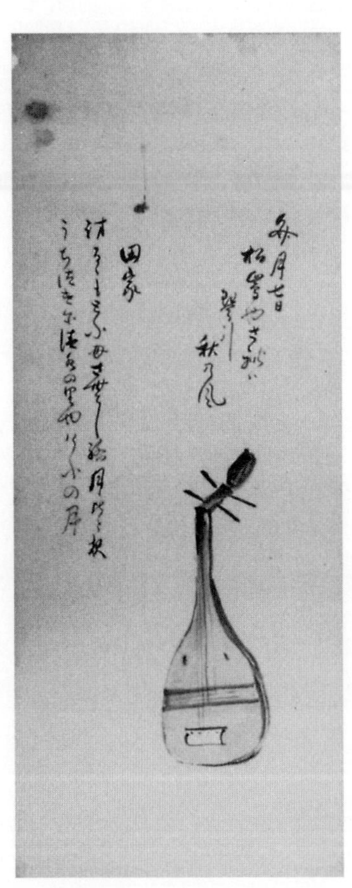

19. Takebe Sōchō (1761-1814)
Lotus Root and Kuwai

Ink and color on paper, 40 1/4 x 10 5/8 (102.2 x 27.1)
Masuda Shōzaburō Collection, Tokyo

The lotus is widely admired in Japan. Aside from its beauty, it has a Buddhist connotation, rising from the mud at the bottom of a pond to blossom in purity, and therefore sculptures of deities are commonly set on lotus-petal pedestals. In addition, the lotus root is eaten in the spring, and makes a delicious addition to a *tempura* dinner. It is primarily in its role as a food source that Sōchō celebrates the lotus root in this haiga, growing in the valley along with *kuwai,* arrowhead bulbs that are eaten at the New Year. The haiku captures the sound of the muddy fields being prepared for the planting of rice:

Ta ya kaesu	Plowing over the paddy?
hetara hetara to	"plish plash"
tani no soko	valley bottom

The long lotus root boldly stretching upwards, the echoing long thin line of calligraphy, and the three little bulbs create one of Sōchō's most dramatic compositions. This thematic combination once again demontrates how haiga can take the most mundane of objects or scenes and give them new vitality.

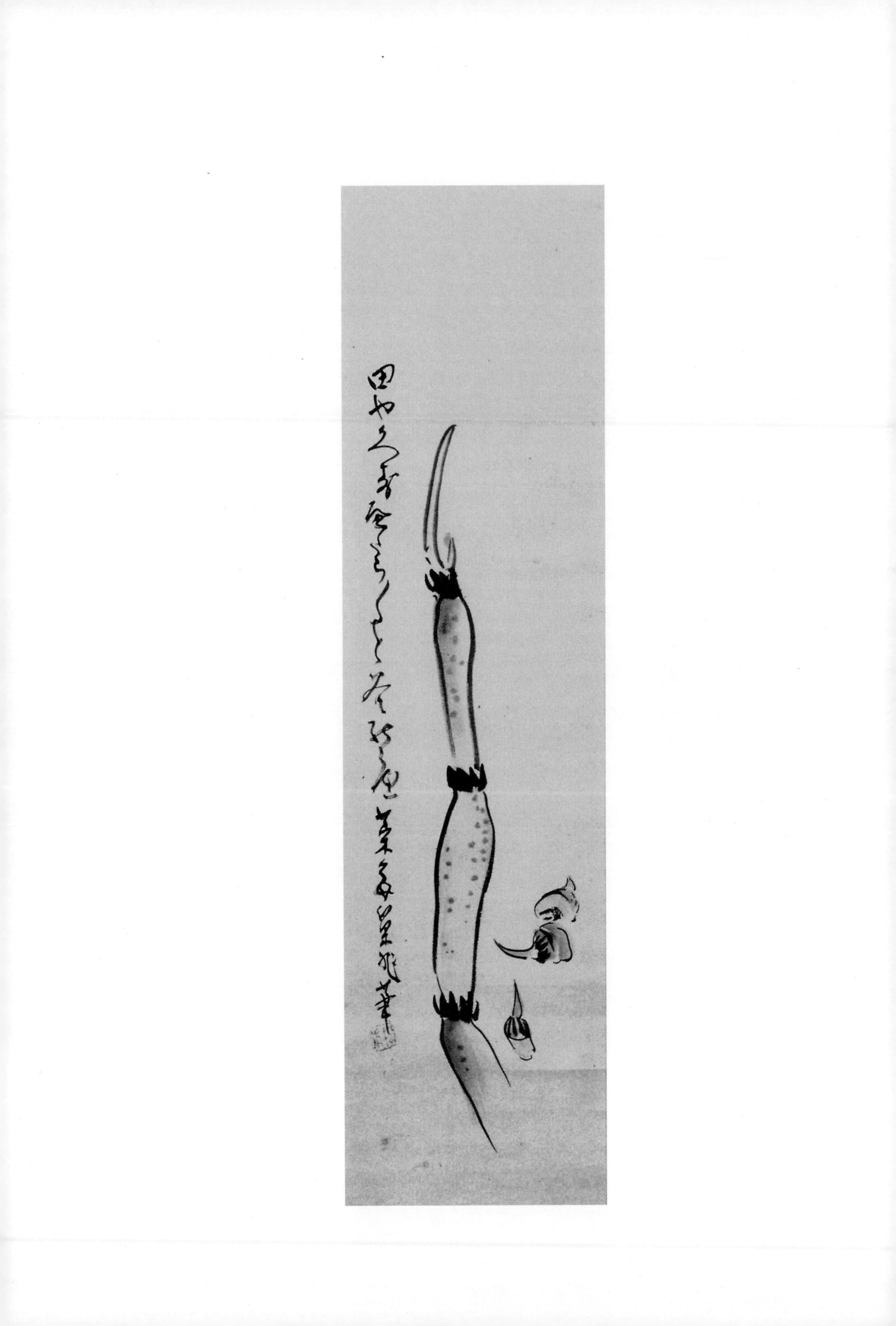

田や[illegible]

20. Takebe Sōchō (1761-1814)
Sixteen Rakan

Ink and color on paper, 50 3/4 x 24 (128.8 x 61)
Masuda Shōzaburō Collection, Tokyo

One of Sōchō's most complex haiga shows an age-old Buddhist subject, the enlightened disciples of the Buddha called *rakan.* These figures are usually portrayed in groups of 16, 18, or 500, and often have strange, humorous faces and poses. Having advanced beyond worldly cares, they can be as eccentric as they please. Several can be identified by their attributes; one has a pet tiger, while another keeps a dragon in a bowl from which it flies out from time to time.

Upon closer examination, Sōchō's figures seem much less cosmic than most *rakan.* Instead of a dragon and tiger, they are accompanied by dogs, fish, and ducks, and they are playing with flowers and incense rather than contemplating Buddhist truths. In fact, they are haiku poets in the guise of *rakan,* a form of art called *mitate.* Sometimes translated as "parody," *mitate* refers to new and often humerous transformations of classical subjects. Sōchō also designed woodblock versions of these figures, labelling them with specific poet's names, so he was clearly poking fun both at the serious *rakan* tradition and at his poet friends. Above the *rakan*-poets are eight haiku, reading from the right:

Bashō ha ni kogoto kakikeri yūsuzumi	On a banana leaf writing my criticisms — evening cool	— *Katsuri (1743-1817)*
Fuyu no hi wa kan no juppo ni amarikeri	Winter day the stork walks ten steps — and then walks some more	— *Yūshō (dates unknown)*
Mikazuki wa mono no magure ni mitaru kana	The new moon suddenly noticed among the distractions	— *Suikei (?-1813)*
Kamiyo yori kono iro mochishi asagao ka	Since the age of the gods have they kept this color? morning glories	— *Taikyō (1763-1828)*
Kokoro hodo sumu mono mo nashi ogi no koe	Compared with mind there is nothing as clear — voice of the reeds	— *Tsunemaru (1750-1810)*
Hotaru-mi ya tsuriai waruki yoru no kasa	Watching for fireflies is not harmonious with an evening sedge hat	— *Utō (1757-1832)*
Ogamaruru asahi to narinu tsuyu no aki	Worshipping the rising sun, it becomes the autumn dew	— *Seibi (1749-1816)*
Michibata ni umarete suzushi aka torii	Alongside the road, giving birth to coolness — red torii gate	— *Takebe Sōchō*

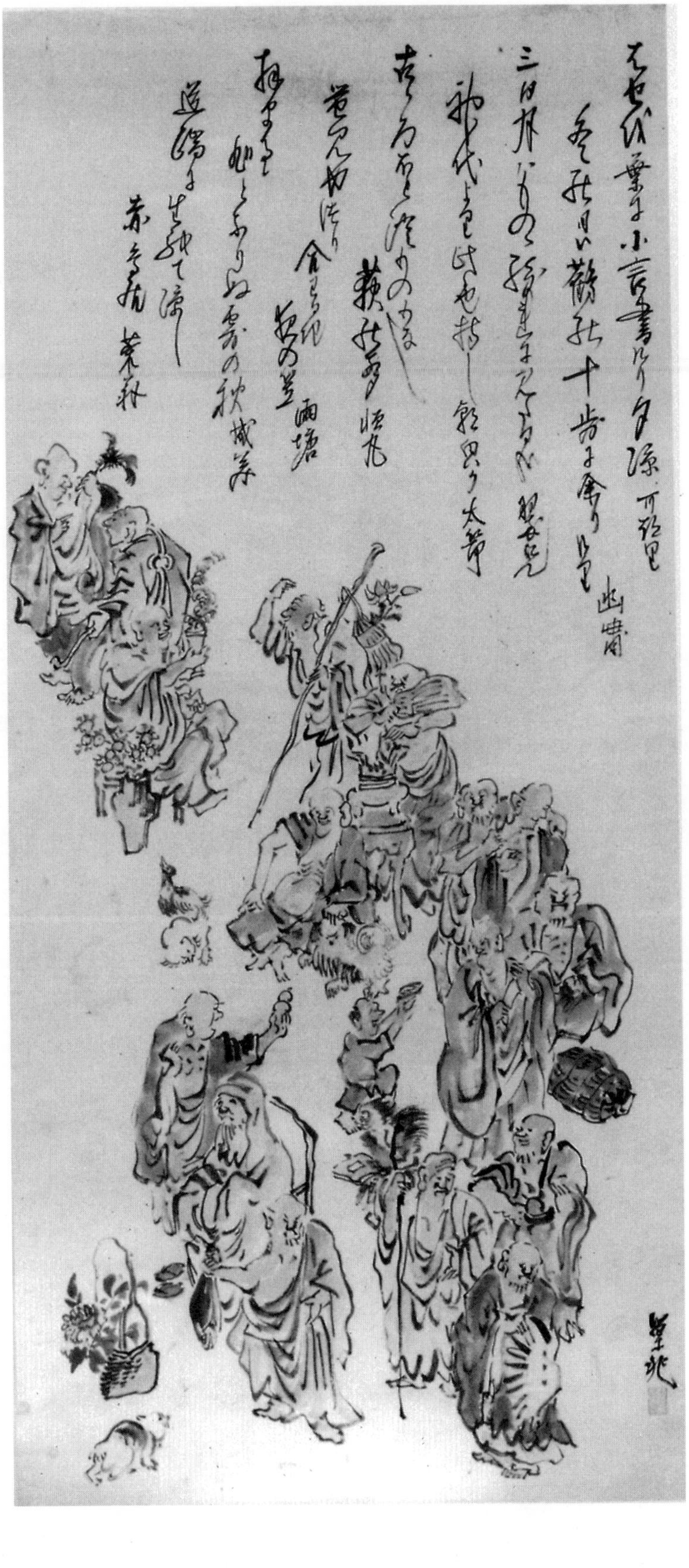

Note: from the left top, the first three poets are Tōkaku (dates unknown), Baiju (dates unknown), and the seated Sogan (dates unknown). Next come Issa (1763-1827) with the staff, Kanpo (Seibi's son, dates unknown) holding a fan, and Bon'ro (a friend of Seibi and Issa, dates unknown) patting a dog. Below them are, from the left, Ichiga (?-1826), Taichiku (1726-1845), and Ippyō (1769-1840); all three are standing behind Sōchō, who is being offered a cup by an attendant. In the lower right are the smiling Rōa (a friend of Seibi, dates unknown), Sharyō (a pupil of Seibi, dates unknown) with the staff, and Shinpi (?-1825) holding his hat. At the lower left are Baku-u (?-1813) with a gourd, the seated Seibi, and Kyūzō (1778-1859) holding a fish.

21. Takebe Sōchō (1761-1814)

Packhorse

Ink and color on paper, 36 3/8 x 11 1/8 (92.4 x 28.3)
Masuda Shōzaburō Collection, Tokyo

Here Sōchō has depicted a packhorse and his owner; their backs are bent with age and labor, but both look feisty as they proceed on their journey. The relationship between the two is strongly articulated, with the man's sedge hat fitted nicely in the space between the horse's hooves. But it is the horse who does the most work, and while his energy turns downwards as he hunches over, his owner strides forth with a determined look. Sōchō has placed his signature and seal amusingly at the horse's rear end.

The horse is loaded with large packs of tobacco, a prized commodity in early modern Japan that was usually smoked in pipes with long stems and small bowls.

Tabako-ni no	Tobacco packs
mare ni hitome mo	seldom seen by people —
kareno kana	withered fields

The tobacco having been harvested, the fields are bare and withered, but the word *kareno* also signifies the lonely chill of autumn with its melancholy mood. The packhorse and his master meet no companions on the roads, and thus Sōchō has added to his lively and somewhat humorous painting a poetic undertone of somber melancholy.

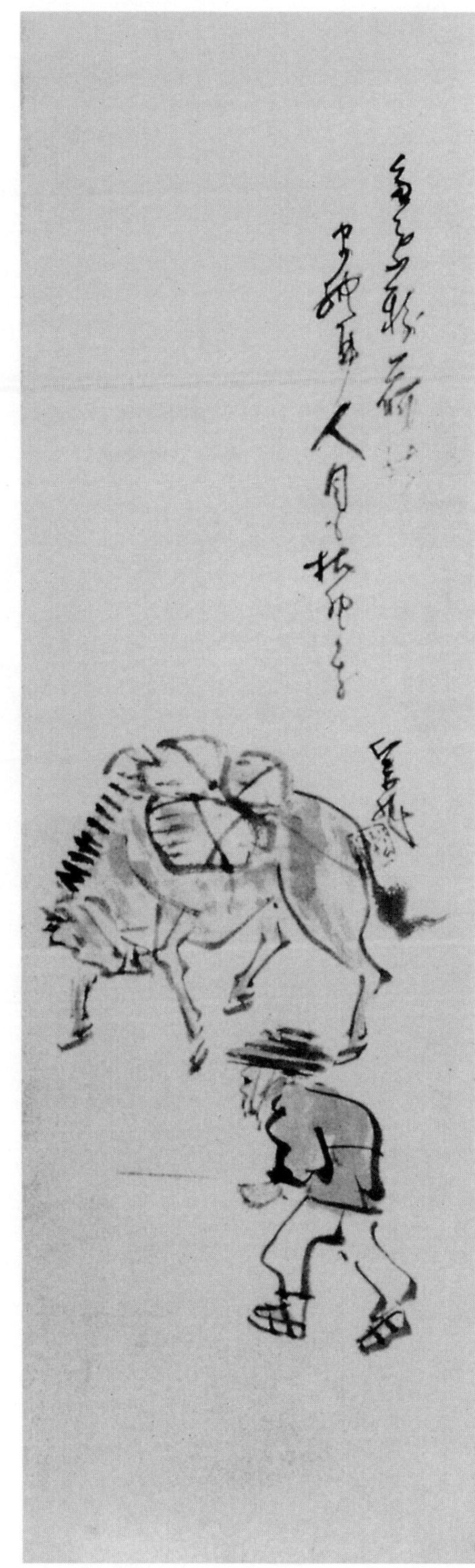

22. Takebe Sōchō (1761-1814)

Yoshiwara Haze

Ink and color on paper, 34 x 11 (86.3 x 28.2)
Masuda Shōzaburō Collection, Tokyo

The figure strolling along in this haiga seems to be wearing two swords. This was an honor allowed by the government only to samurai, in recognition of their importance as warriors. However, during the long period of peace under the Tokugawa regime (1600-1868), samurai were no longer needed for their military prowess, and became gradually transformed into civil officials. This was a role that they did not all appreciate. Those who lacked either the talents or the ambition to serve in a bureaucracy, or were set loose by feudal lords who could no longer pay them, became *rōnin,* masterless samurai with no real home and often with nothing but their pride to sustain them.

Samurai, as the highest class, were not supposed to visit the Yoshiwara, the famous area just at the edge of Edo that was set aside for the brothels, bath houses, and tea houses of the so-called "floating world." Therefore samurai were sometimes depicted in early woodblock prints visiting the Yoshiwara incognito, with their faces hidden behind basketlike hats. Here Sōchō has shown a samurai walking, or perhaps we should say staggering, along a path in the countryside outside the Yoshiwara. The time of day seems to be very early in the morning after a night of pleasure--or is it imagined pleasures that animate the haiga? The brushwork is extremely relaxed and the inktones are as moist as the samurai who, none the worse for wear, looks off into the distance:

Waga io wa	My hermitage
Yoshiwara kasumu	the Yoshiwara haze —
shiwasu kana	last month of the year

One important aspect of haiku is the ability of the poet to identify with the subject matter of his poem; here we can sense Sōchō becoming the samurai, looking off towards the Yoshiwara from his home in Sekiya. In this case, the poem could be translated:

From my hermitage
the Yoshiwara is in haze —
last month of the year

So we may ask whether the Yoshiwara is covered in mist, or whether in fact the samurai's home *is* the mist, the unreality of the Yoshiwara in which life seems to float in the haze as the year comes to an end.

我庵ハよし原
二[illegible]
[illegible]
[illegible]

23. Takebe Sōchō (1761-1814)

Reeds

Ink on paper, 13 1/4 x 20 1/4 (33.7 x 51.6)
Masuda Shōzaburō Collection, Tokyo

One of Sōchō's most powerful paintings is a close-up depiction of waterside reeds. They bend and twist in powerful diagonals, as though the viewer were peering through them at the silvery moonlight. And that is exactly what is suggested in Sōchō's haiku:

Dore kara to	Where did it come from?
ogi no tonari ya	next to the waterside reeds —
nochi no tsuki	late autumn moon

Sōchō places the poem at the upper right, but his signature and seal are in the midst of the painting's composition, as though they themselves might represent the moon next to the reeds. Or might the moon be reflecting in the water, a Zen symbol for illusion?

The brushwork is broad and primarily wet, with some blurring and fuzzing of the ink, suggesting a moist autumn evening. Sōchō paints with great tonal variations, so that single strokes of the brush are transformed from deep black to many shades of grey. However, in the top center where two leaves cross, they both become dry and ultimately transparent, as if shimmering with light. These *ogi* are common waterside plants, yet they take on an almost magical intensity in Sōchō's dramatic visualization.

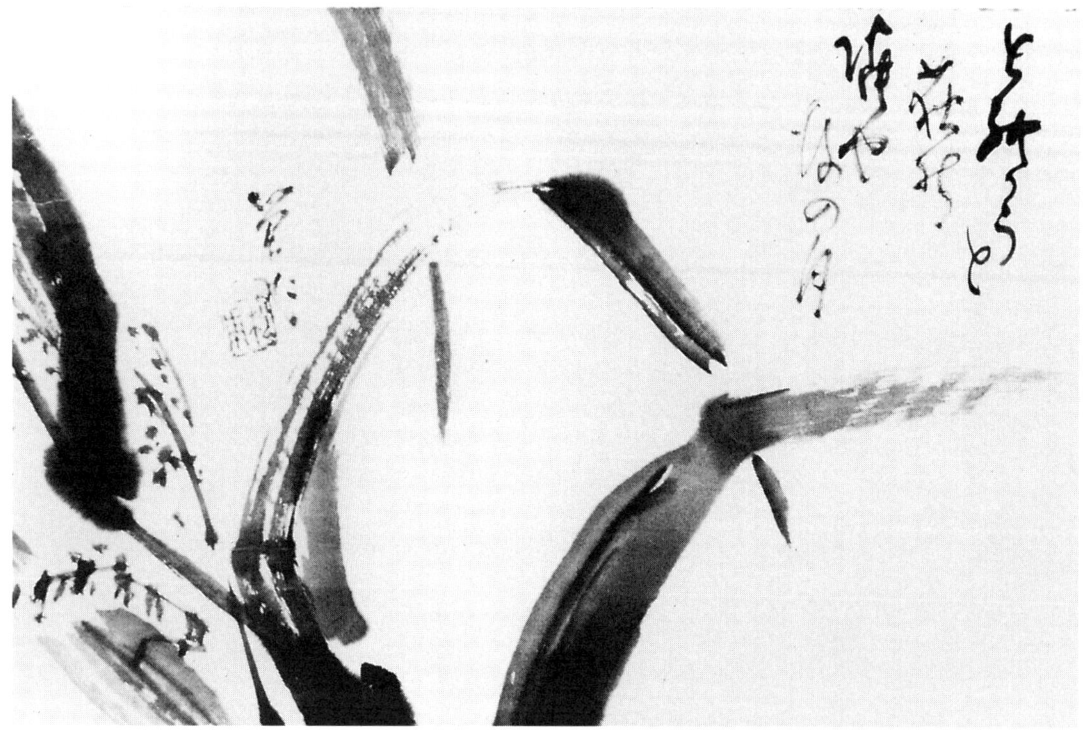

24. Takebe Sōchō (1761-1814)
Old Couple

Ink and color on paper, 48 1/2 x 6 1/2 (123.3 x 16.7)
Private Collection

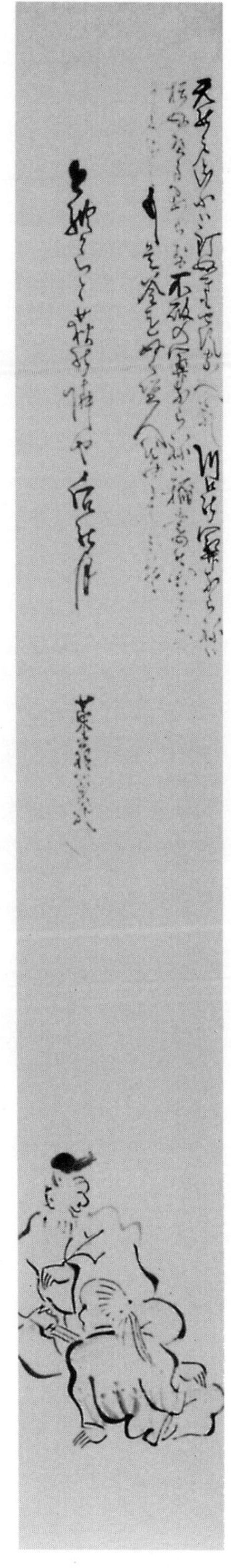

Sōchō has here used the same poem as on his haiga *Reeds* for a completely different subject, an old couple relaxing. This time he adds an introduction, referring to the moon as the entrance to the Milky Way:

> The "Heavenly Door" has no pincers, nor do people.
> Since it is not Kawaguchi Barrier, it will not rot.
> Since it is not Fuwa Barrier, it will not emit lightning.
> A thief who would pull out this fish-trap will not be permitted to do so.

The meaning seems to be that the moon is unbound and cannot be stolen, but is available to be enjoyed by people of whatever age and social standing. In some ways, this introduction echoes the Chinese phrase that begins the *Mumonkan,* a collection of Zen kōan: "The great way has no gate."

After his introduction, Sōchō's haiku remains the same:

Dore kara to	Where did it come from?
ogi no tonari ya	next to the waterside reeds —
nochi no tsuki	late autumn moon

Why did Sōchō portray the old couple, instead of the reeds as in the previous scroll? As discussed in the essay on Sōchō, he paints as if he has just "peeped in" to their a small house, in order to present the human response to the late autumn moon. The two works show two main aspects of haiga, one directly evoking an experience such as watching the moon, and the other depicting those who are partaking in the experience.

To make this second approach more effective, Sōchō has chosen a format and style quite different from the haiga of *Reeds.* Here, instead of a horizontal composition, the scroll is tall and thin, with a great deal of empty space. Rather than powerful rough brushwork in ink, the old couple is depicted with gently curving lines and light colors. In order to help us envision a different level of the meanings in his poem, Sōchō has created an entirely different haiga.

25. Takebe Sōchō (1761-1814)

A Journey in Honshū, 1799

Ink and color on paper, 10 7/8 x 283 (27.6 x 727.1)
Spencer Museum of Art, University of Kansas; Gift by Exchange of H. Tully Moss

In its early manifestations in Japan, the handscroll format was primarily used for narrative painting, with artists taking advantage of the fact that such a scroll could be gradually unrolled to create the effect of a "moving picture." However, Sōchō has here utilized the format to present a series of interrelated paintings and poems that move the viewer through the months and seasons in various parts of Honshū, the largest Japanese island. At the end of the handscroll, Sōchō writes that it was composed at an inn at Zenkō-ji in Nagano Prefecture on the twentieth day of the ninth month of 1799.

The first image, allotted a good deal of space, shows two huts and two pine trees at Sekiya nestling along a curve of the Sumida River. After two poems about plum blossoms, Sōchō's fourth haiku celebrates another spring image:

Uguisu no yane kara oriru hatake kana	The warbler comes down from the rooftop to the field

Next comes a great variety of subjects; this scroll could make an exhibition by itself. The themes include Sōchō's home at Sekiya, two travelers, a memorial stone, a mountain monk, a child's dove toy on wheels, two women going to a picnic, a pine tree at Nikko, a priest of Kyoto's Yoshida Shrine, the warrior Soga brothers, a fortune teller, pilgrims in winter, musical instruments, bush clover, three figures in a boat on the Sumida River, and, finally, two people at a kitchen stove.

After this long series of paintings and poems (not illustrated), the final haiga of the scroll focuses upon a pleasure that could easily be overlooked:

Toshi kurete hi o taku ni sae omoshiromi	At year's end even making a fire is delightful

The enjoyment here is not only warming up during the coldest month of the year, but also preparing rice cakes for the New Year's feast soon to come. In this way Sōchō concludes the seasons of the year while at the same time bringing forth the cycle of life that is endlessly renewing.

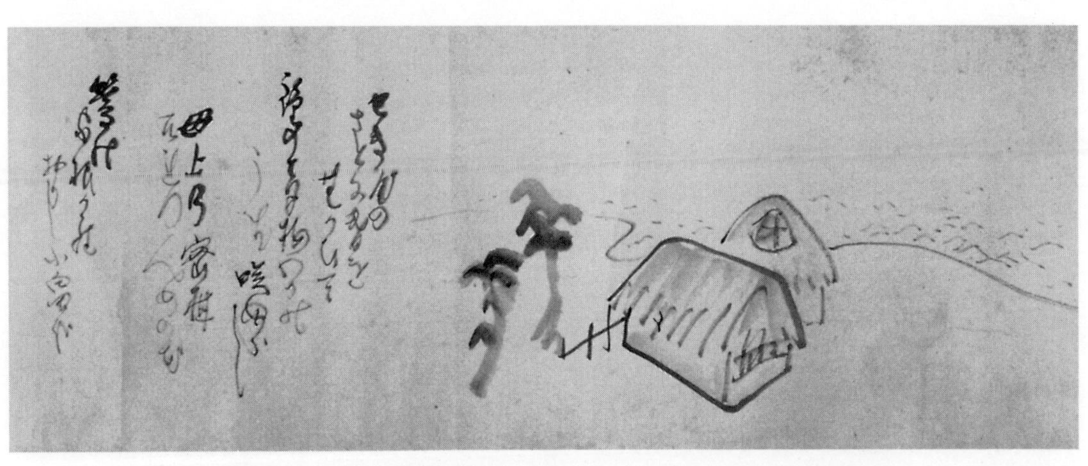

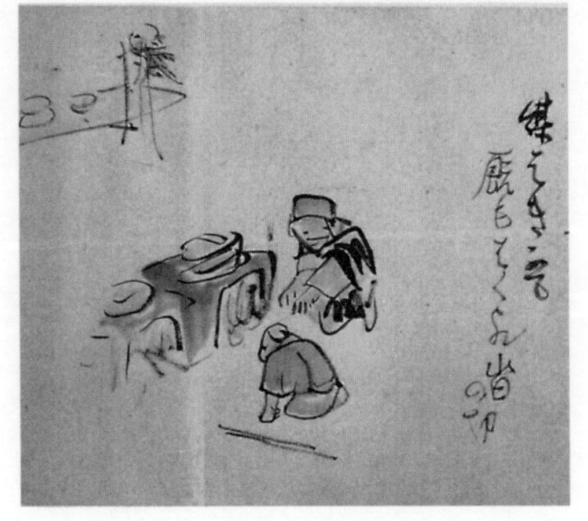

26. Takebe Sōchō (1761-1814)
Discussions under a Mosquito Net

Ink and color on paper, 13 3/8 x 21 3/8 (34 x 55.8)
Masuda Shōzaburō Collection, Tokyo (color illustration, cover)

One of Sōchō's most delightful haiga shows four old men, two women, and a baby clustering under a mosquito net, just like a slumber party. The poem was also used on Sōchō's screens for the sixth month (see Cat. No. 18).

Susuki kara ka no deru yado ni tomarikeri	From the pampas grass mosquitoes came into the inn where I stayed

Sōchō has arranged the figures in a semicircle extending into a horizontal like the shape of a ladle. The lumpy form of the final body is echoed in a kind of visual parody by the lamp and the sedge hat. In back, the women seem content to sleep, but the baby looks on in wonderment as the four old geezers smoke, wave a fan, and chat. The purpose of haiku and haiga is to show ordinary moments and make them special: the scroll evokes the full flavor of summer at a Japanese inn.

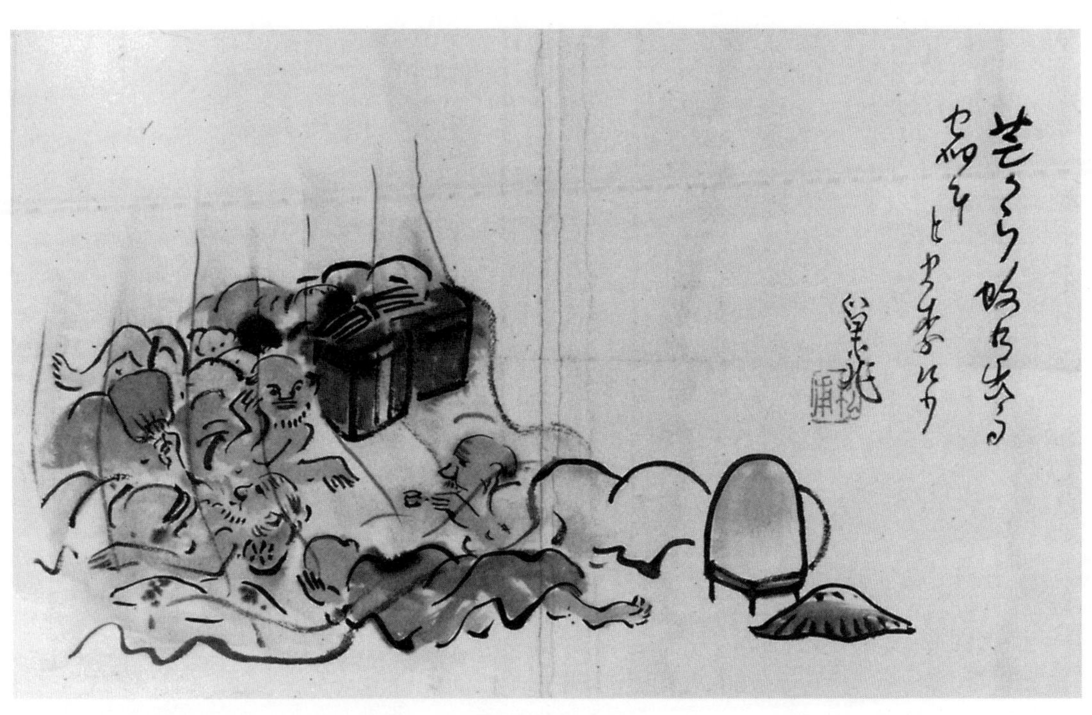

27. Takebe Sōchō (1761-1814)

Shōhaku on a Bull

Ink and color on silk, 44 1/2 x 14 (113 x 35.5)
Masuda Shōzaburō Collection, Tokyo

Shōhaku (1443-1527) was one of the major *waka* and *renga* poets of his time, and helped to lead the way towards the beginnings of haiku poetry. It may be that Sōchō also enjoyed the fact that one of Shōhaku's closest friends was a *waka* poet also known as Sōchō (1448-1532), although his name was written with different characters. This earlier Sōchō joined Shōhaku and their teacher Sōgi (1421-1502) to create two of the most famous Japanese linked-verse sequences, "Three Poets at Minae" and "Three Poets at Yuyama," each consisting of one hundred verses alternating between the three masters.

In his poems, Shōhaku was able to combine the refinement of courtly aesthetics with the rustic flavor of a Buddhist hermit. Here he is shown riding a bull with a somewhat bemused expression, possibly inebriated, and clearly unconcerned about where he is going. Perhaps he is viewing his beloved peonies, one of which hangs next to the head of the bull. Sōchō has brought the image of Shōhaku forward on the silk by painting a light grey wash around the figure.

The work is not, strictly speaking, a haiga; the long inscription consists of an prose excerpt praising wine from Shōhaku's *San'aiki (Records of Three Loves):*

> As for wine, I've tried Chinese nectars; I've sought out everything from the wonders of thick white sake from Kyushu, chrysanthemum wine from Kashū, and sake from Amano, to the thinnest and least refined of drinks; I've dispersed a thousand worries in a single cup; I've mended my spring clothes with this feeling of complete inebriation, keeping out the wind and cold and reaching an unexpected old age; I will frolic on awhile longer, and return my heart to the beginnings of my youth.

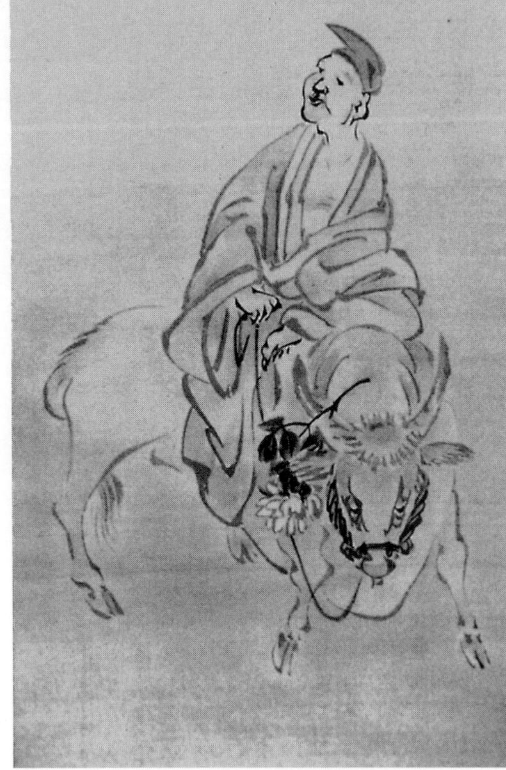

28. Takebe Sōchō (1761-1814)

Inscription by Tsuji Rangai (1758-1831)

Strange Figure

Ink and color on paper, 46 1/8 x 10 1/4 (117 x 26.1)

Masuda Shōzaburō Collection, Tokyo

One of Sōchō's most amusing and memorable paintings is also one of his most mysterious. Who is this strange figure?

Before trying to answer this question, we can consider the poem:

Tsuki ni e o sashitaraba yoki uchiwa kana	If you put a handle on the moon — a good round fan

Although here inscribed by Sōchō's poet friend Rangai, this verse was originally composed by one of the first major figures in the transition from *renga* to haiku, Sōkan (1465-1553). Credited with inventing a form of linked verse called *haikai renga,* Sōkan has also been admired for studying Zen, retiring from his life as a samurai, and living as a monk at his modest hermitage. Some of Sōkan's poems show a lightness of touch that may seem surprising in a man of artistic and spiritual perception, but humor in Japan is not seen as an absence of depth, but rather a different way of exploring that depth. In this case, if the moon can never be grasped, how can it be given a handle and become a fan?

To the question of who this strange figure may be, the most obvious answer would be Sōkan, since many haiga show the poet rather than an image from the poem. But Sōkan was a monk, and this figure is not. Furthermore, he is looking rather dismayed, and the fan he is holding is not the round Chinese-style *uchiwa* type mentioned in the haiku, but the more common Japanese folding fan. With his body composed of wriggling lines, his toes curled up in concentration, and his long nose, he almost looks like a *tengu,* a form of semihumorous Japanese demon. Could this be a poet of Sōchō's generation, trying to figure out the meanings in Sōkan's poem, or wishing to compose a haiku as delightful and multilayered? Might Sōchō and his friend Rangai be adding one more layer of humor to Sōkan's famous verse?

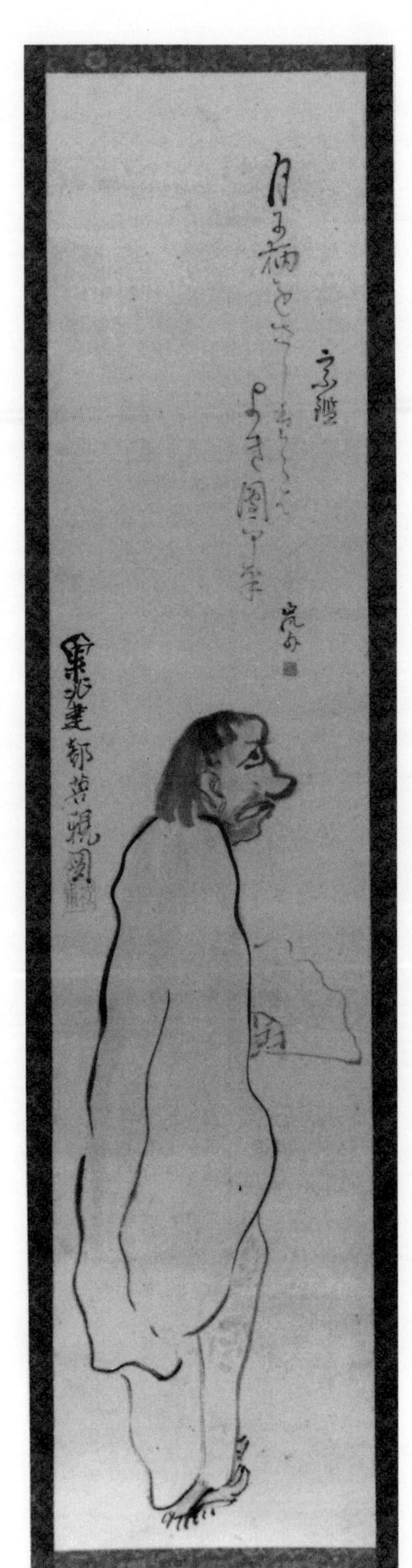

29. Takebe Sōchō (1761-1814)

Inscription by Kameda Bōsai (1752-1826)

Charcoal Seller, 1804

Ink and color on paper, 37 x 11 (94 x 28)

Masuda Shōzaburō Collection, Tokyo

Sōchō's circle of friends included people from all walks of life, and he was especially drawn to artists and poets of many schools and backgrounds. One of his closest friends was his brother-in-law Kameda Bōsai, a well-known scholar-poet-artist of Edo. Bōsai had begun his career as a dedicated teacher, but his own Eclectic School of Confucian philosophy promoted the idea that each person should find and follow his or her own path, rather than accept standard doctrines from a teacher. The Japanese government found this kind of eclectic Confucianism dangerous and declared it heterodox, eventually causing Bōsai to lose his school and students.

Sōchō and Bōsai lived near each other and socialized a great deal. As a result of their friendship, Bōsai inscribed a number of Sōchō's paintings with his Chinese-style poetry, which contrasts with haiku in several ways. Instead of three lines in Japanese of 5, 7, 5 syllables, traditional "regular verse" is completely balanced, with either 5 or 7 Chinese characters in every line. In addition, this form of poem is composed of an even number of lines, most often four or multiples of four.

In the final month of 1804, Sōchō and Bōsai combined forces to portray a charcoal-seller making his living in the cold of winter. Although this is no longer haiga, Sōchō's depiction is relaxed and informal, following his haiku-painting style. The old man leans forward as if to reach out to a buyer of his charcoal, trying both to make a sale and to keep warm in the chilliest month of the year. Bōsai's quatrain mentions a specific brand of charcoal, *Choshin* (literally, "bird-firewood"); was this a brand name of the time, or Bōsai's own invention? The translation is by the scholar Jonathan Chaves:

> "Bird-wood" fills his single basket:
> Just pecks and pints — Ah! This chilly scholar!
> Beneath a mournful sky of windswept snow,
> He'll sell you balmy vapors of the Spring!

In a roundabout way Bōsai may well be referring to himself in this poem. He had become impoverished by losing his school, and he survived by filling requests from ordinary people as well as fellow scholars for his poetry, calligraphy, paintings, and book prefaces. Surely he would not have missed the irony that since he used *sumi* (ink made from charcoal) in his writing and painting, he was not far from the man selling *sumi* (the charcoal itself) on the streets. And the "bird-wood" being sold is close to his own art name of Bōsai, which literally means "Phoenix Hall." Therefore this portrait of a chilly scholar can create warmth in the imaginations of those who understand his work.

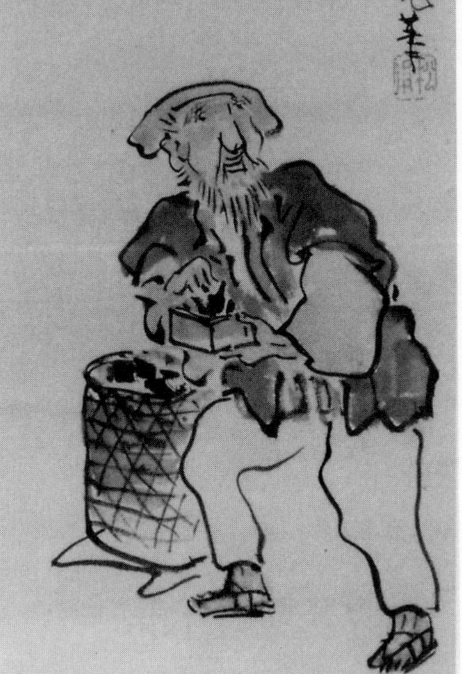
甲子晩歳　文晁筆
爲薪歳一簣升斗
分寒〻士風雪蕭寥
霄賣與陽和氣
甲子十二月鵬齋醉題

30. Takebe Sōchō (1761-1814)

Inscription by Shikatsube no Magao (1753-1829)

Courtesan and Apprentice

Ink and color on silk, 12 1/2 x 17 (31.8 x 43.1)

Masuda Shōzaburō Collection, Tokyo

In the early to middle nineteenth century, a form of "crazy poem" (*kyōka)* became wildly popular in Japan, particularly in the bustling city of Edo. Although haiku remained important, many clever and stylish poets turned to five-line humorous verses, which were often parodies of the elegant courtly *waka* tradition. One of the leading *kyōka* masters of Edo, Magao was a merchant who quit his business to become a professional poet, a role he took seriously. In his final years he even appeared at poetry gatherings dressed in the clothes of a nobleman, and his verses are less topical and satiric than others of the day, maintaining more refinement within their humor. As one of the most successful *kyōka* poets of the early nineteenth century, Magao became a well-known member of the "floating world" of artists, printmakers, poets, and courtesans.

Here Sōchō has created not a haiga but a *kyōka*-painting by elegantly portraying the highest class of courtesan, the *tayū,* with her young attendant. The courtesan is dressed richly but informally, with a subtle pattern of gold painted on her under-robe. Her long hair is lightly fastened and then cascades down her back like that of a noblewoman from the Heian period (794-1185). She has put down her fan; opening her lacquer letter-box, she peruses what must be a missive from her lover. Her expression, however, is not joyful, and Magao's poem adds to the bittersweet mood:

Uguisu wa	Even when
haru no tsukai ni	the warbler comes as
kitemo mada	spring's messenger
fubako no himo no	the cords of the letter-box
musubōru koe	resound with gloomy notes

Like most *kyōka,* this poem is very difficult to translate because it is full of puns and double meanings, such as the "cords" of the box and "chords" of music, as well as both written and musical "notes." We can be sure, however, that the cheerful voice of the warbler is not matched by the voice within the letter.

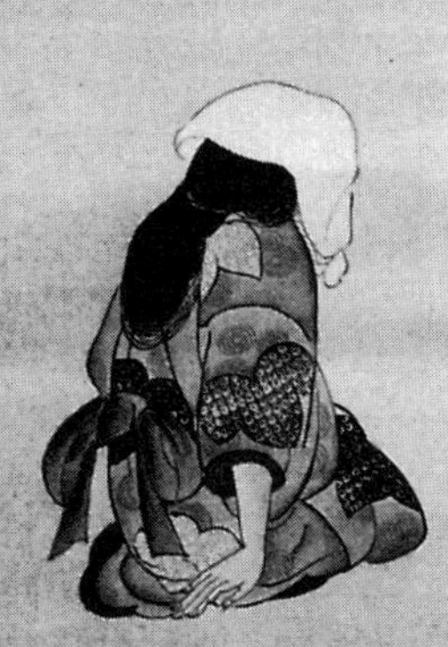

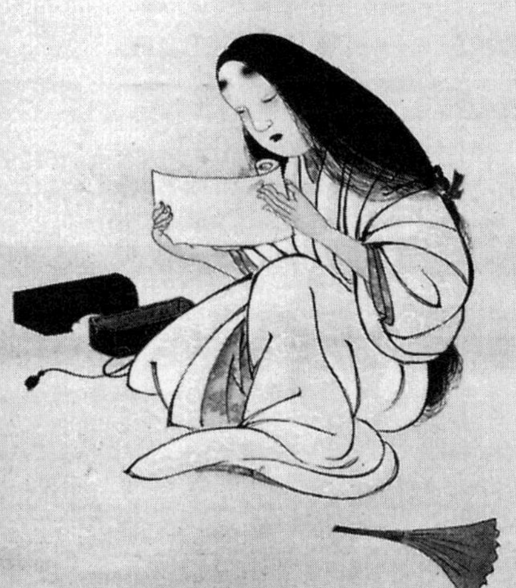
建部英親

31. Takebe Sōchō (1761-1814)
Bird-keeper

Ink and color on paper, 18 1/2 x 21 1/4 (47.2 x 54)
Masuda Shōzaburō Collection, Tokyo

Although the majority of Sōchō's paintings are haiga, he was also an accomplished artist in other styles of painting. Those of his works that are without inscriptions include delicate paintings of beautiful women in the *ukiyo-e* tradition, larger-scale figures in a somewhat eccentric style, and carefully painted smaller works such as this depiction of a young man feeding his pet birds.

The handsome, rather effete youth pictured here is a *wakashū,* an elegant young man who often becomes the focus of homoerotic desire. He is beautifully dressed in the fashion of the later seventeenth century, an era of special glamour and stylishness. One might almost mistake him for a woman but for his hairstyle and the shaved area of his head. He is feeding a warbler, while a skylark awaits his turn in the next cage.

By placing the *wakashū* in the center of the composition, Sōchō ensures that he will be the focus of attention and admiration. The style of the brushwork is appropriately elegant and refined, the colors are restrained, the pose is graceful, and the brushstrokes are much more smooth and silken than in Sōchō's haiga. In particular, the lines defining the youth's garments, curving over his shoulders, overlapping at his throat, and ballooning at his knees, show the artist's great skill. These lines swell and attenuate so gently that they do not detract from the focus upon the *wakashū;* we are led to feel that we are peeking in at the youth's private life as he tenderly feeds his warbler and skylark. Yet, just as the singing birds are caged, so may be the young dandy in the hothouse world of sexual favors.

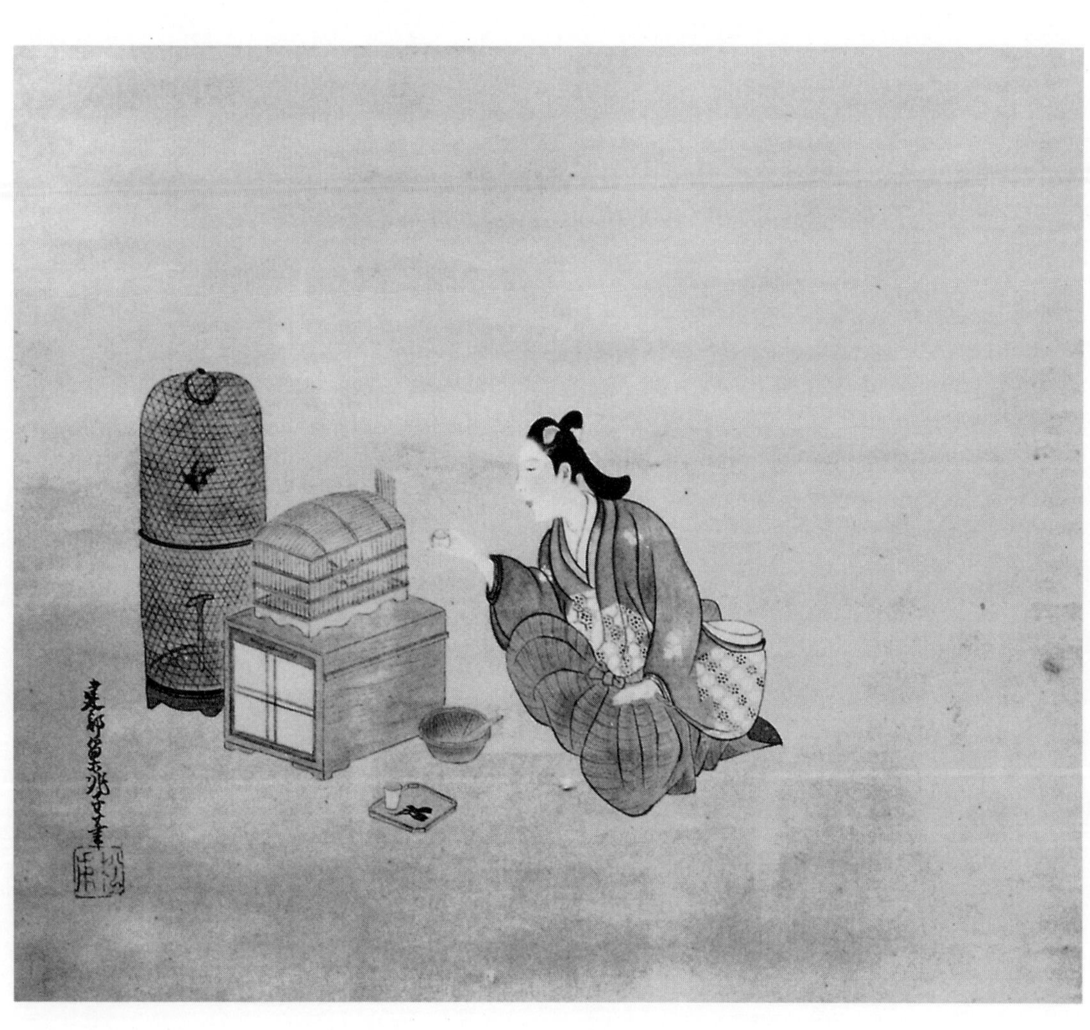

32. Takebe Sōchō (1761-1814)

Portrait of Bashō, 1892

Woodblock print, mounted on scroll, 24 3/4 x 12 (62.9 x 30.6)
Masuda Shōzaburō Collection, Tokyo

The history of this print began a hundred years before it was created. To commemorate the 100th anniversary of Bashō's death in 1793, Sōchō painted a portrait of the master. Although he could never have seen the great poet in person, Sōchō based his depiction upon earlier paintings, including the traditional robe and hat that are seen in many portraits of Bashō.

For this portrait, Sōchō did not paint in his usual relaxed haiga style. Instead, he chose to portray Bashō as naturalistically as possible, suggesting how the master might have looked to his friends and disciples. Compared with other portraits of Bashō in this volume, Sōchō's conception is the most detailed and elaborate. He utilized delicate lines, careful brushwork, muted colors, and even some shading in the robe and hat to add a sense of volume. The gentle expression on Bashō's face is enhanced by his modest seated pose with his hands folded above his waist. It is clear that Sōchō held Bashō in great respect, and his painting served as homage as well as commemoration.

When Bashō's 200th anniversary approached, Sōchō's portrait was so highly admired by lovers of haiku and haiga that it was printed in woodblock form and issued on November 11, 1892. This high-quality printing was certainly fortunate, for the original portrait is now lost, and probably no longer exists. Only the woodblock version remains to convey the reverence of a fine haiku poet-artist to the greatest master of his craft.

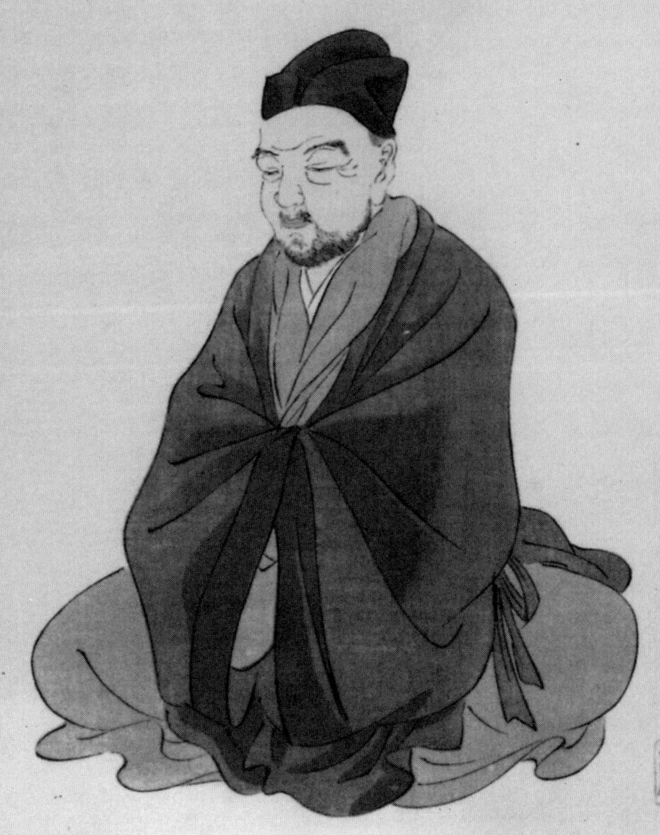
梁兆建部英親謹畫
松浦

33. Takebe Sōchō (1761-1814)

Two Book Illustrations

Woodblock prints; two-page spreads; upper: 9 x 11 3/4 (22.8 x 30), lower: 8 7/8 x 11 1/2 (22.7 x 29.2)
Masuda Shōzaburō collection, Tokyo

Illustrated woodblock books are perhaps the least understood and appreciated forms of art from early modern Japan. Although a few seventeenth-century volumes were set in movable type, the huge numbers of Chinese characters used in Japanese texts made this method cumbersome. Thereafter books were almost all hand-carved from blocks of cherrywood. Since both text and images were carved in the same way, it was easy and natural to add pictures to books. Because Sōchō was highly admired as painter, poet, and connoisseur, he became very active in the world of woodblock books and publishing. Not only were many of his haiku printed, but he also edited several anthologies of poetry, and added pictures to other volumes.

Books of haiku poetry occasionally featured a single master, but more often were compendia of groups of poets, with one or more editors choosing the verses to appear in the book. When the books were successful, they often came out in several volumes, usually over the course of a few years.

The fifth volume of the *Tsuru shibashū (Crane's Turf Collection),* issued in 1801, contains one of Sōchō's most delightful images (upper right). A group of haiku masters including Sōchō had visited the temple of Zenkō-ji in Nagano Prefecture, and a group of local poets came out to greet them. The image recalls paintings of tribute being offered Chinese emperors, and Sōchō adds to the humor by his caricatures of the faces of the traveling poets, one of whom may well be himself.

Six years later in 1807 Sōchō designed an image for *Hanagoeshū (Flower's Voice Collection),* this time showing a monkey trainer and his performing monkey (lower right). The man looks serious and determined, while the monkey is gesturing in theatrical grandiloquence. The human is certainly the master of the animal, but who seems to be having the most fun?

While both woodblock prints are based upon a strong compositional diagonal, they show two different uses of line. For the poets, Sōchō preferred loose curved strokes, giving a feeling of rumpled relaxation. In his picture of the monkey trainer, however, the lines are sharp and angular, creating a more tense and dynamic image. The signature and seal add a visual accent to the composition; Sōchō's seal here reads *Yamato eshi,* "Japanese painter," showing that he is identifying himself as an artist in the native tradition instead of the more idealistic Chinese style popular at his time. By showing these scenes with sympathetic humor, Sōchō is also clearly establishing his aesthetic as the illumination of daily life.

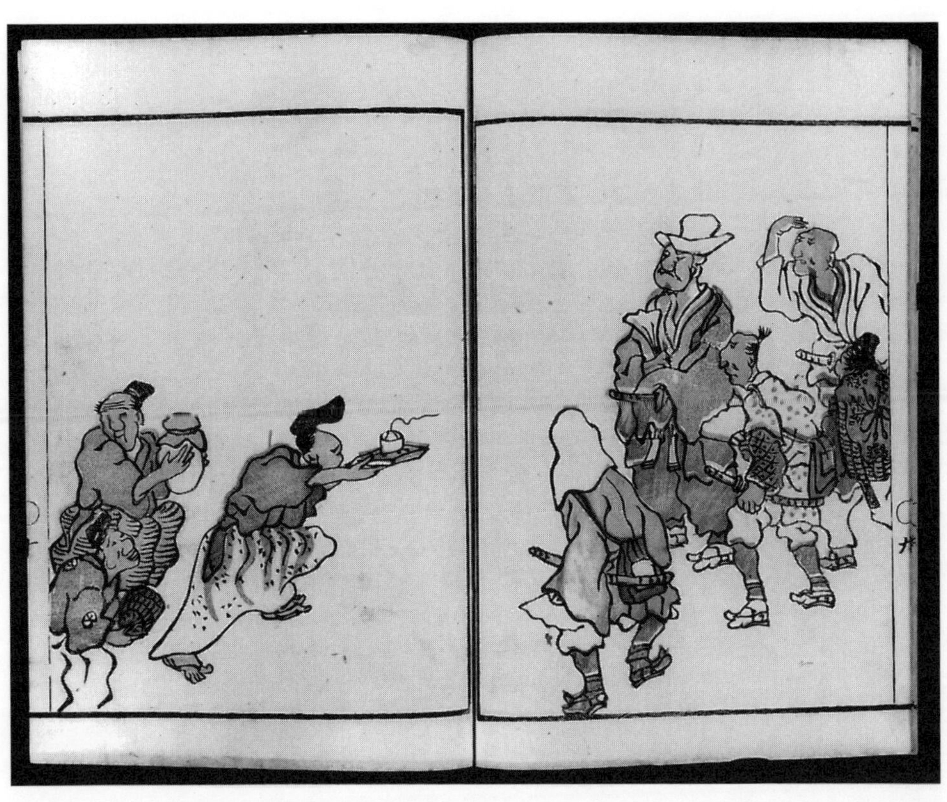

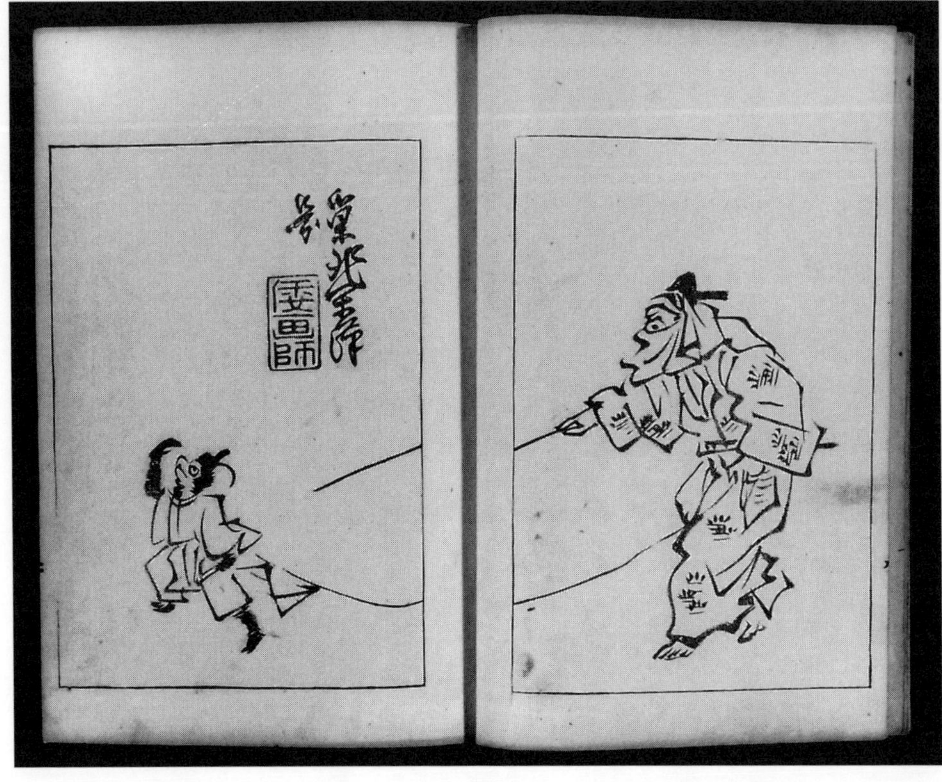

34. Kobayashi Issa (1763-1827)
Garden Butterfly

Ink on paper, 11 1/4 x 14 3/4 (28.6 x 37.6)
Private Collection

The third of the great haiku masters after Bashō and Buson, Issa is particularly known for his compassion for all living creatures, including fleas and mosquitos. His own life as the son of a farmer was tragic; his mother died when he was two, and all his four children died in infancy or childhood.

Issa spent years wandering all over Japan, absorbing the sight and sounds of city and countryside. His poem about a butterfly in the garden suggests both the beauty of nature and the futile pursuit of happiness:

Niwa no chō	Garden butterfly
ko ga haeba tobi	as the baby crawls, it flies —
haeba tobu	crawls close, flutters on

The image of the young child chasing the butterfly that always flutters just beyond reach can be taken for a Buddhist lesson in not grasping. Issa's contemporary, the English poet-artist William Blake, sang the same truth:

He who binds to himself a joy
Does the winged life destroy
But he who kisses the joy as it flies
Lives in Eternity's sunrise

Issa would certainly have agreed, but the haiku spirit suggests rather than proclaims. That may be why Issa depicted neither the child nor the butterfly in his haiga. Perhaps the movement of the calligraphy may suggest the flight of the butterfly, but there is no further need to pictorialize — if we chase the butterfly in our minds, it is gone.

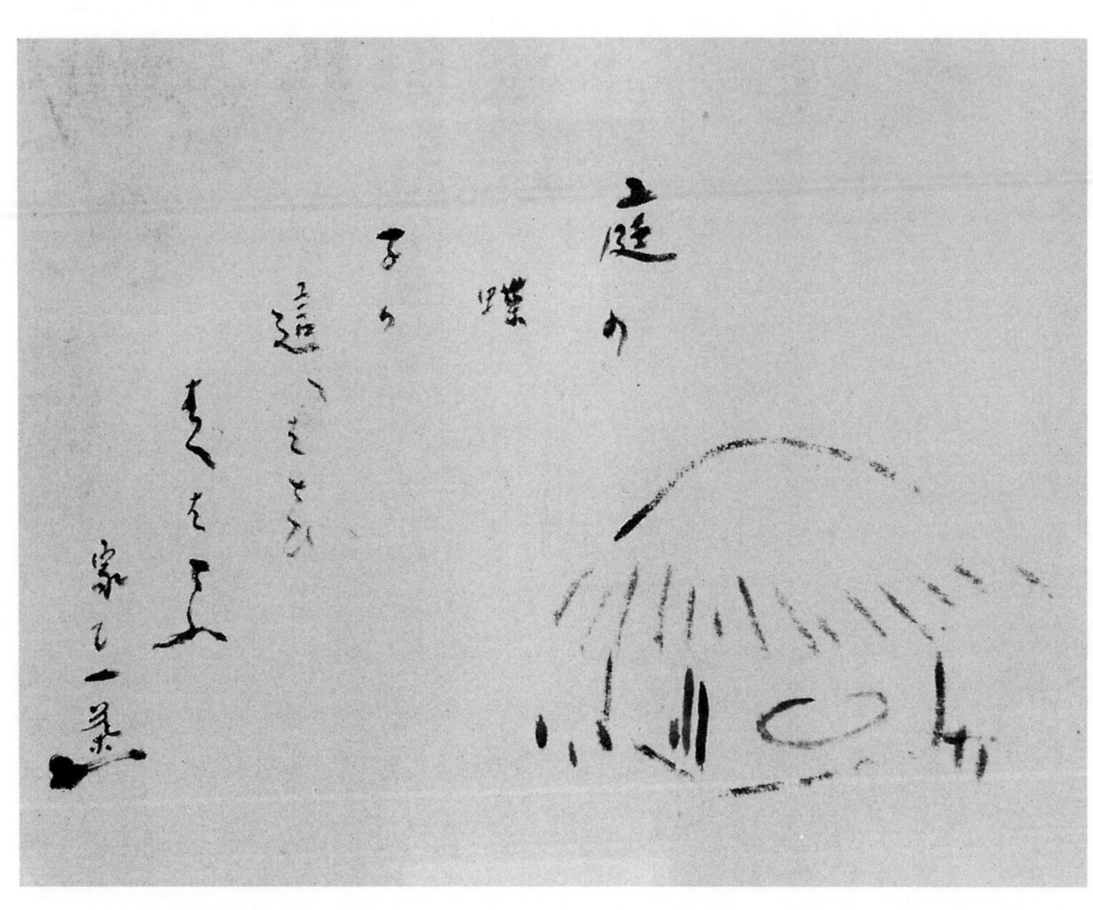

35. Inoue Shirō (1742-1812)

Self-Portrait

Ink on paper, 45 x 10 7/8 (114.4 x 27.6)
Private Collection

Shirō was a doctor specializing in gynecology in the city of Nagoya, situated between the new capital of Edo and the old capital of Kyoto. His true love was haiku and haiga, and along with several talented friends he created a circle of poets and artists that made Nagoya a major artistic center. Although Shirō generally followed Buson in both poetry and painting, he also created a new tradition of haiga that empathized extreme simplicity and evocative description.

Iro mo ka mo	No color or scent
nakute hana miru	when flower-viewing —
kazahana kana	stuffy nose

This is surely one of the most unusual self-portraits ever painted. Instead of a clearly defined figure, we are offered a strange shape that is difficult to understand. Is it the profile of a face with whiskers hunched over a stubby body? Shirō is certainly being self-depreciating, and his poem echoes this playful mood. The word *kazahana* is written as "stuffy nose," but with different characters it can also mean "snowflakes." When Shirō has caught a cold he cannot appreciate the flowers, but pure white snowflakes are also like tiny blossoms that have no color or scent.

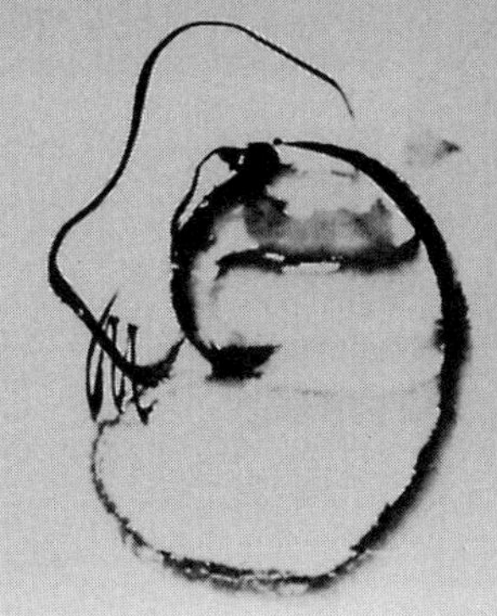

36. Inoue Shirō (1742-1812)

Cuckoo

Ink on silk, 10 5/8 x 15 (27 x 38)
Private Collection

In haiga, does a simple or a complex image more easily suggest multiple meanings? This is not an easy question; details and elaborations can particularize a scene, pinning it down to a specific meaning, but sometimes they can also suggest further ideas, feelings, and relationships. In general, the haiga by poets are more minimal than those by professional painters, and this seems to have been a conscious choice even by those who had a high degree of painterly skill. This image, for example, needed only five brushstrokes, but it shows Shirō's complete command of grey washes of ink on silk without outlines, a difficult technique to master. But skill is surely not the impression that Shirō sought to convey; rather, he would have preferred us to sense the flight of the cuckoo as it calls out in the moonlight. And Shirō's multiple meanings can then be activated by the relationships between image, calligraphy, and poem.

In Japan, the cuckoo is the harbinger of summer; poets (and lonely lovers) might stay up all night waiting to hear its first cry. The cuckoo is also one of the few birds to sing as it flies, and Shirō paints it, beak open, swooping in a slightly curving diagonal across the top left of the composition. The calligraphy of the poem forms an echoing diagonal, creating a sense of movement that suffuses the scroll.

The character for "moon" was written boldly at the beginning of the third column of the poem. Because this word retains some of its original pictographic crescent-shaped form, we may sense the cuckoo actually flying past the moon. The grey shading of the bird also helps to define the sense of silvery light on the slightly toned surface of the silk. In these ways Shirō is able to create the strong presence of the moon without having to depict it in painted form.

Kyo koborete	Instead of home —
suzushiki tsuki no	the cool moonlight's
mushiro kana	straw mat

The haiku does not mention the cuckoo, but suggests a summer night. One interpretation might be that rather than staying in his house, the poet is out in the moonlight. But has he taken his straw mat with him, or does the moonlight create a mat for him? And has he been waiting for just this moment when the cuckoo calls?

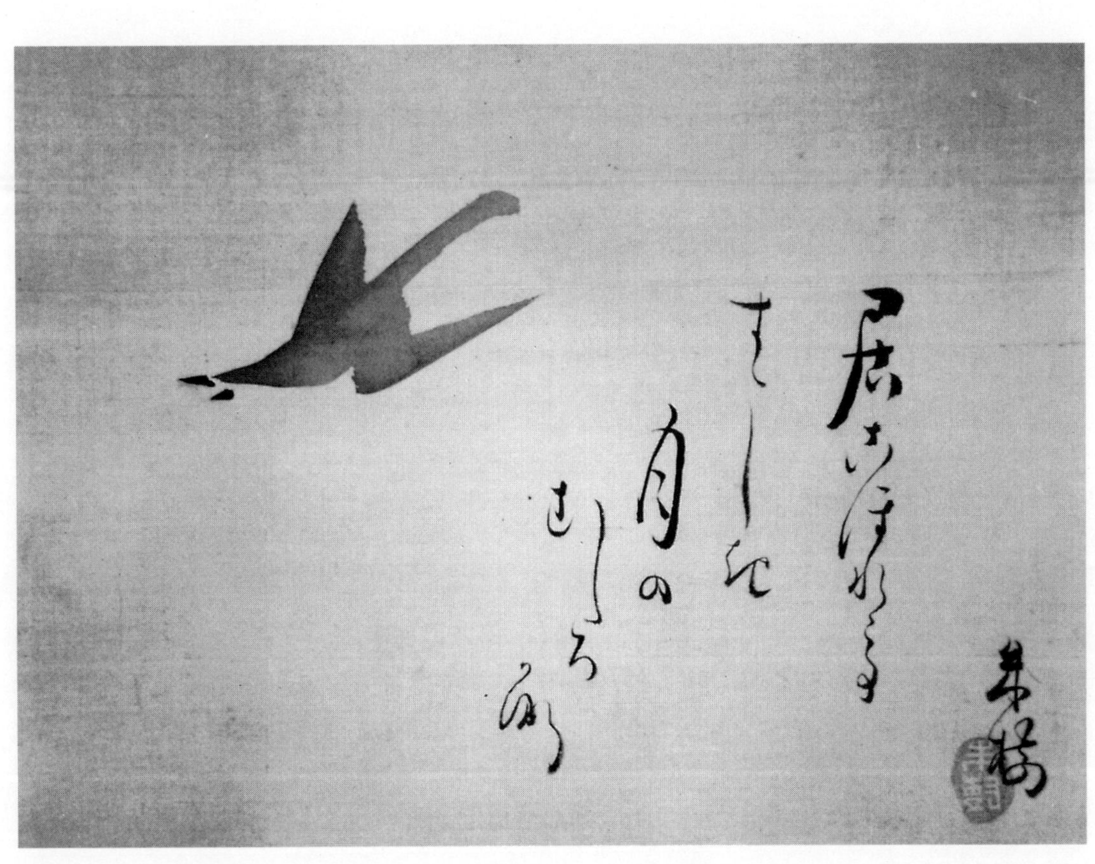

37. Inoue Shirō (1742-1812)
Moon

Ink on paper, 12 1/4 x 19 5/8 (31 x 50)
Private Collection

Shirō has here evoked the form of a mountain with a single brushstroke. This seems so easy, couldn't anyone do it? Let's look more closely. The contour moves up from Shirō's signature at the lower left, curves, moves back downwards, curves again, and bends gently as it descends to the lower right. By creating a smaller and then a larger diagonal, it gives a sense of movement to the composition. Furthermore, it is not limited to one tone of ink, instead revealing darker and lighter greys within its single stroke. Dividing the total space roughly in half, this brushstroke allows just enough space for the haiku in the upper right.

Yorozu-yo ya	Through the ages
yama no ue yori	rising above the mountains —
kyō no tsuki	tonight's moon

The final word of the poem, *tsuki,* both means and pictorializes the moon. Shirō slightly separates this word from the rest of the haiku, enlarges it, and bends it at an opposite diagonal to the shape of the mountain: the moon rises in a blend of painting, poetry, and calligraphy.

All this, and yet the work looks as if it had been created with no thought or care at all. This is the secret of haiga — to combine boldness and grace without any effort. Seemingly simple, haiga requires a perfect touch.

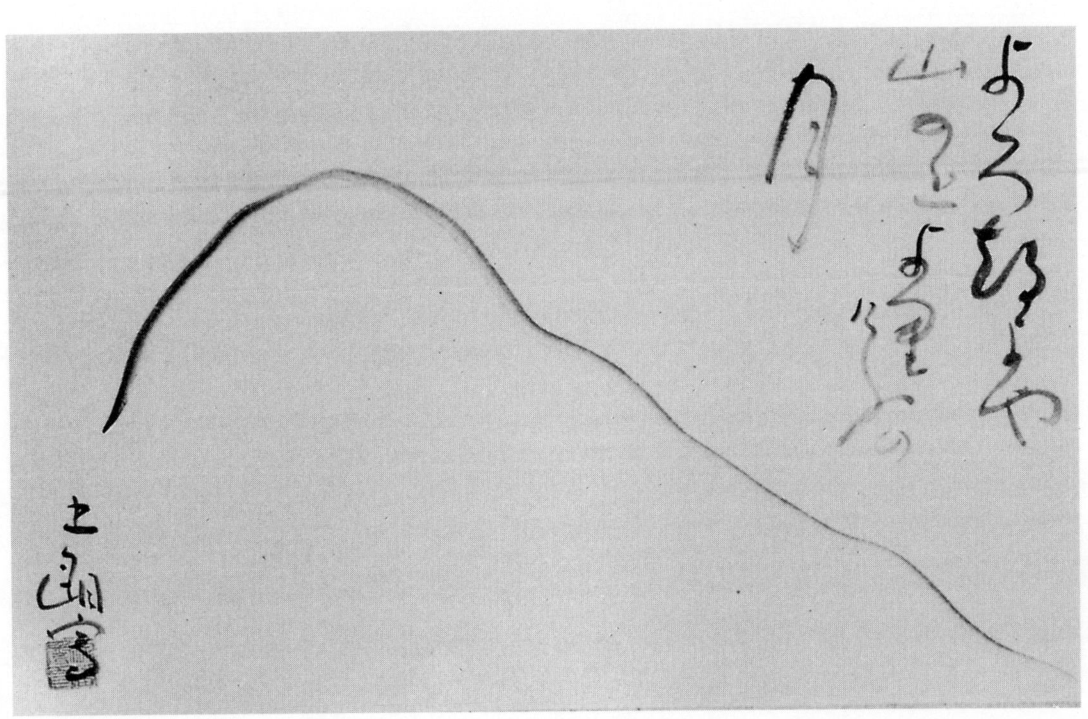

38. Fujimori Sōbaku (1758-1821)

Dawn of the Thirteenth Night

Ink on paper, 45 x 11 (114 x 28)
Private Collection

Sōbaku was a merchant friend of Shirō who became a Buddhist priest. He enjoyed creating haiga as well as haiku, being especially noted for his figure paintings. Here he has shown an old couple at their little brazier. The caricature of the faces adds a touch of humor, one of the characteristics that often appears in both haiku and haiga, helping to keep them from becoming banal or pretentious.

The title Sōbaku gave this scroll relates to the Japanese passion for moon-viewing; the thirteenth night of the ninth month was considered to have the brightest moon of the year.

Kakugo shite	Once you know
yami wa akarushi	that darkness is also bright —
jūsan ya	the thirteenth night

From the painting we might not be able to guess the meaning of the poem, and vice-versa, since the two arts bring forth images that complement, rather than describe, each other. We certainly need not insist upon one composite meaning in the total work, but there are certainly several ways in which the interaction between text and image can be seen. On the simplest level, the old couple is willing to go out in the dark night because they know the moon will be bright. On another level, their brazier creates enough light for them, and they do not really need the moon. More broadly, in the world of haiku as in Zen, brightness is in the eyes and mind of the beholder.

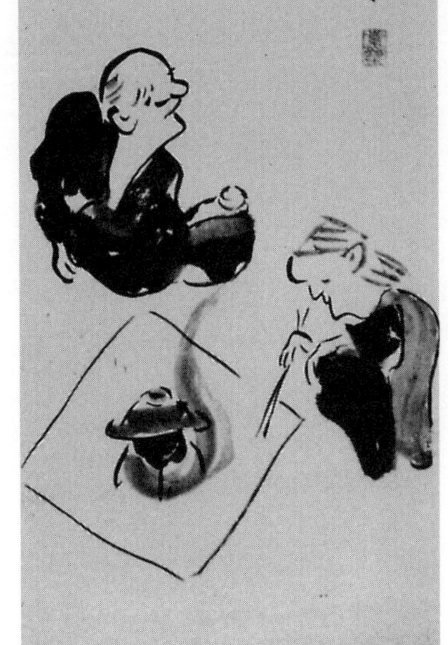

39. Suzuki Nanrei (1775-1844)

Inscription by Kameda Bōsai (1752-1826)

Portrait of Bashō

Ink and color on paper, 34 1/8 x 10 3/4 (86.7 x 27.3)

New Orleans Museum of Art, Anonymous Donor

Most nineteenth century haiku poets revered Bashō as the greatest master of the genre, and artists therefore received many requests to paint portraits of him. This example comes from more than a century after the poet's death; it was created by Nanrei, an artist of the naturalistic Shijō school of painting. He shows Bashō seated next to his traveling case, eyes closed and gently smiling. Is he dreaming of his most famous poem? By Nanrei's day, it had already become known to every schoolchild in Japan:

Furu ike ya	Old pond —
kawazu tobikomu	a frog jumps
mizu no oto	the sound of water

A poetic inscription for this portrait was requested from the scholar-calligrapher Kameda Bōsai. This was somewhat unusual, since Bōsai was celebrated for his poetry and calligraphy in Chinese style, rather than in the Japanese haiku tradition. Nevertheless, Bōsai complied with the request, adding a touch of wit by his parody of Bashō's famous verse. Is he suggesting that by the early nineteenth century, there was no longer a true master like Bashō ?

Furu ike ya	Old pond —
sono go tobikomu	after jumping
kawazu nashi	no frog

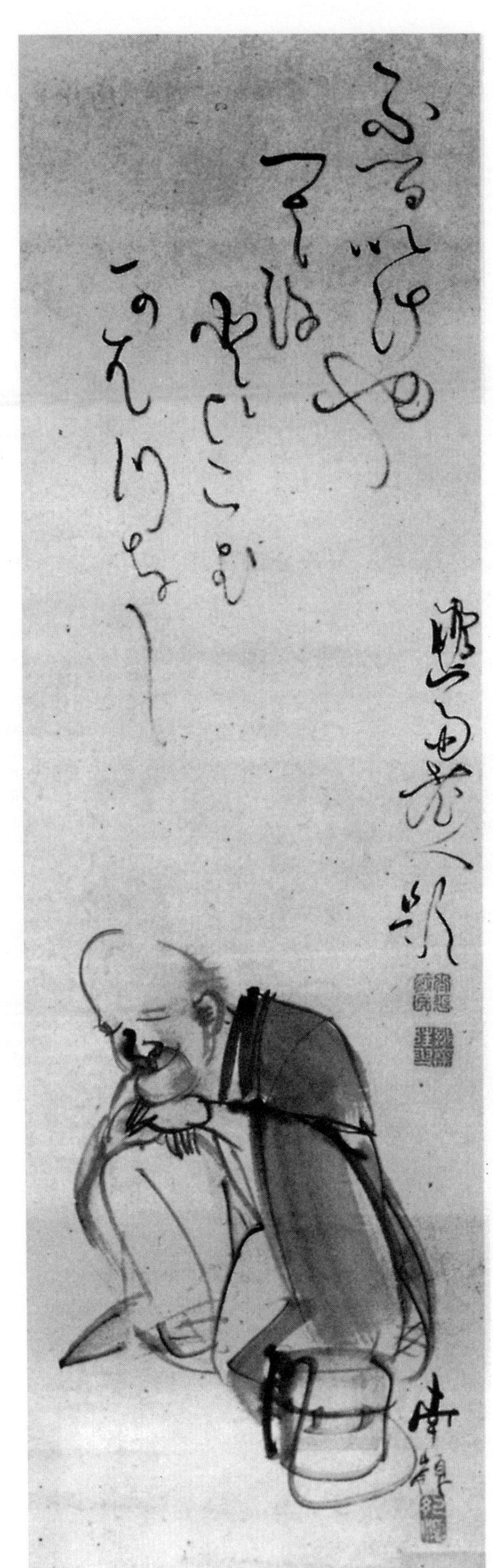

40. Suzuki Nanrei (1775-1844)

Haiku by many poets; calligraphy by Negahara Shōhō (dates unknown)

Farmer and Two Boys in Harvested Fields, Autumn 1831

Woodblock print diptych, 15 1/4 x 43 (38.7 x 109.3)

Private Collection, Japan

Among the most fascinating, if little-studied, works of later Japanese art are the large-scale haiga *surimono* created by artists of many different schools of painting during the eighteenth and nineteenth centuries. *Surimono* are privately issued prints, usually commissioned by poetry clubs, with images by leading artists and poems by members of haiku groups and associations. While the smaller-size *surimono* by *ukiyo-e* artists such as Hokusai are celebrated, the large poem-prints by other painters, such as important masters of the Shijō school, are still almost unknown. The scholar Louise Virgin is completing a thorough study of this field that will surely surprise and delight all those who enjoy Japanese art and poetry.

This exhibition may whet the appetite for the future by including one *surimono* diptych, with a rustic autumn image by Nanrei that extends over the two prints. A farmer is out in the rice fields with two boys who play on a raised path between the paddies. The man carries a net in his hands, probably for catching *shigi* (snipe) that he would then carry home in the basket on his back. One of the boys is brandishing a limestick used for catching insects and small birds.

The poems bring forth the mood of the season. The first haiku in each poem section is by a famous poet, usually the teacher or revered associate of the other contributing haiku poets whose verses follow. Special attention should also be given to the last poem in each section. The following translations are by Dr. Virgin.

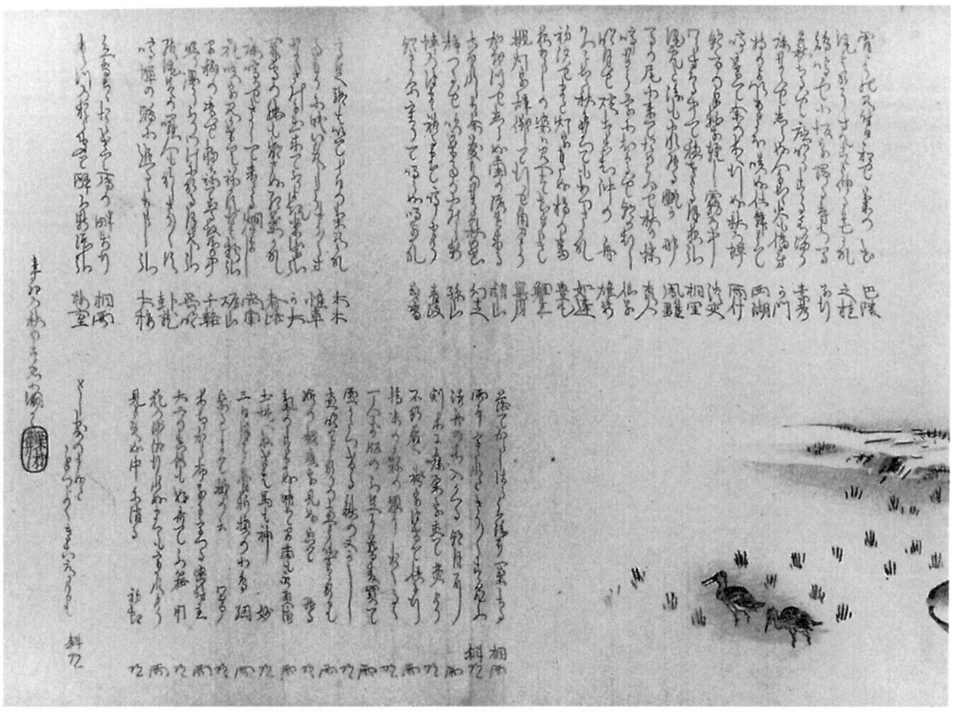

The first poem in the first poem section (upper right corner) is by Narita Sōkyū (1761-1842):

Meigetsu wa
nai hō ga yoshi
kikumi kana

As for the full moon,
so much better without it —
chysanthemum viewing

The final haiku in the first group is by Tsuruta Takuchi (?-1846). It refers to the porters who made their living carrying people across rivers, hoping that their burdens would not be too heavy:

Kawagoshi no
rippa ni watasu
sumō kana

It went so well
crossing the river —
a sumo wrestler!

The final poem of the third group is by Morimura Hōgi (?-1862):

Hagi ni kite
shizuka ni naru ya
uma no hae

Arriving at the bushclover,
they grow quiet —
horseflies

The first poem in the fourth group at the top left is by Sakurai Baishitsu (1769-1852). His reference to the custom of hunting insects and small birds with *mochizao* (gluey limesticks) is echoed in Nanrei's image of the young boy.

Mochizao ni
neji chigiraruru
mukuge kana

Twisted up
on the limestick —
Roses of Sharon

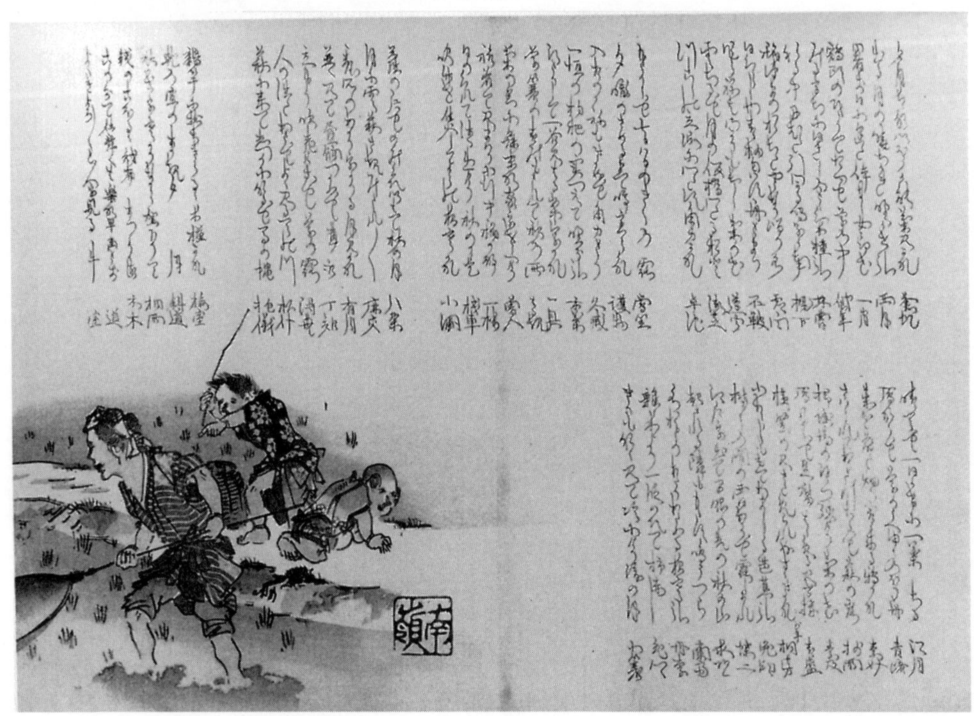

41. Nakamura Hōchū (active c. 1790-1813)
Inscription by Utei (dates unknown)

New Year's Revelers

Ink and color on paper, 17 3/8 x 22 7/8 (44.2 x 58.3)
New Orleans Museum of Art; Museum Purchase, Women's Volunteer Committee Fund

New Year's Day is the most important holiday in Japan, signifying a new beginning. In the old calendar, it occurred somewhere between late January and early March, signaling the beginning of spring and the chance to search for the first plum blossoms. One could also enjoy the *Manzai* dancers who went from house to house at this festive season, singing and playing on a small drum. This haiga was probably painted as a New Year's gift, and it is inscribed by the poet Utei:

Nigiyakana	Born with
umaretsuku nari	liveliness and merriment —
ume no hana	blossoms of the plum

Hōchū was an artist of the decorative Rimpa school, which featured fluent brushwork combined with a strong sense of decorative design. One special feature of the school was the use of merging tones, when ink, water, or color was applied freely over a painted area not yet dry. The result, called *tarashikomi,* creates an agreeable fuzzing and mingling of tonal effects, as shown in the dancer facing us on the left.

This kind of haiga, painted by a professional artist, represents the mainstream of Japanese art more than the modest works of poets such as Issa and Shirō. Nevertheless, Hōchū's humorous depiction of the dancers adds a flavor that well accords with the unpretentious spirit of the finest haiga; the poetry, calligraphy, and painting enhance each other to create the happy spirit of the New Year.

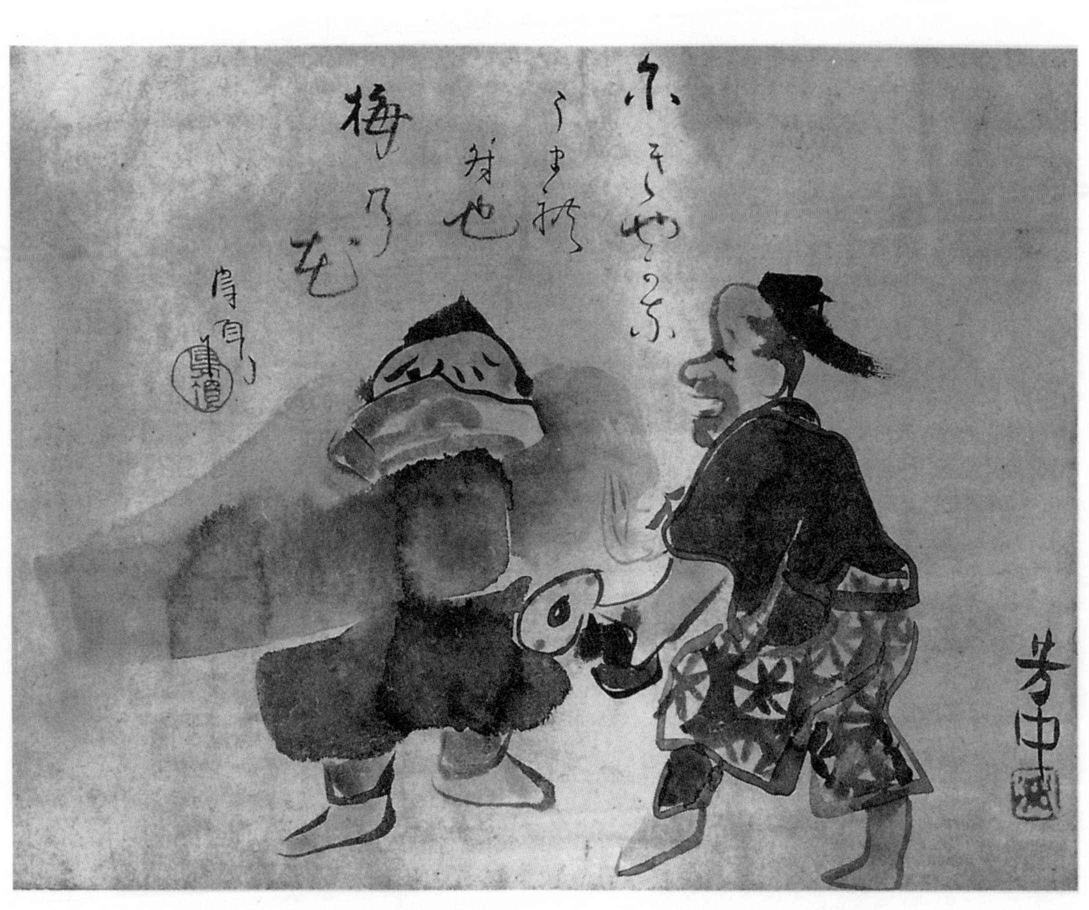

42. Sakai Hōitsu (1761-1828)

Flower and Willow World

Ink on paper, 38 x 11 (96.2 x 28.3)

New Orleans Museum of Art, Gift of Kurt and Millie Gitter

The "Flower and Willow World" was the realm of the courtesans, who lived in the special "licensed quarters" outside Edo called the Yoshiwara. Surrounded by ricefields, the Yoshiwara contained the brothels and tea houses that were celebrated in paintings and woodblock prints by such masters as Suzuki Harunobu and Kitagawa Utamaro. This "floating world" of transient pleasures also attracted Sakai Hōitsu, the second son of a *Daimyō* (lord). A sophisticated aesthete, Hōitsu gave up much of his birthright (and governmental responsibilities) to become a master painter and poet. Most of his scrolls and screens are painted in the bold and decorative Rimpa tradition, but he occasionally created haiga in a more restrained style.

This scroll is the first of a set of twelve representing the twelve months in the Yoshiwara. The large angular calligraphy of the title contrasts with the smaller, more delicate and curving calligraphy of the haiku poem on the left.

Ganjitsu ya	New Year's Day —
sate Yoshiwara wa	and now the Yoshiwara
shizuka nari	is quiet

New Year's Day was the only time that men absolutely had to stay with their families, and so the Yoshiwara was uncharacteristically silent. Hōitsu painted a modest image, depicting only the roofs of three houses, with three birds flying above. But the weight of the title will not let us forget the activities of the Yoshiwara, the world of desire that could be stilled only one day a year.

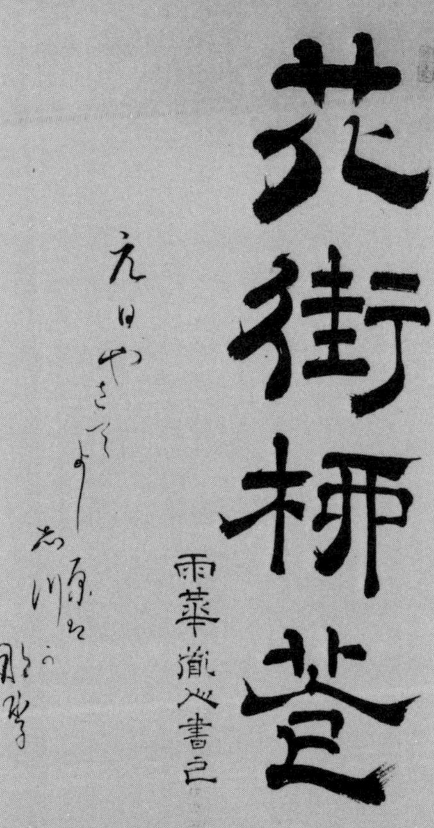
花街柳巷

43. Sakai Hōitsu (1761-1828)

Niwaka Festival

Ink and color on paper, 38 x 11 (96.2 x 28.3)

New Orleans Museum of Art, Gift of Kurt and Millie Gitter

The eighth scroll of Hōitsu's set depicting twelve months in the Yoshiwara celebrates the *Niwaka* festival that took place in late summer. Setting out or carrying inscribed lanterns, male and female courtesans paraded around the Yoshiwara, stopping to perform *Niwaka* dances on stages they wheeled around with them. This festival was occasionally depicted in woodblock prints, but it is rare to see it in painted form.

Compared with the previous scroll (Cat. No. 42), this haiga shows the Yoshiwara in a much more festive mood. Hōitsu has portrayed the courtesans holding up their lanterns while a dancer in a *shishi* (lion) mask dominates the parade under the full moon. Once again, however, the artist has given most of the space to calligraphy and poetry. The large character says *Niwaka,* and to its left there is a prose introduction, with the haiku below to the right.

Although it comes year after year, every time the sound of the lion dancers is heard it's wondrous again, as they wind through the pleasure district:

Shishi no za ni	Returning to take
naoru ya tsuki no	the lion's place, the moon
ondotori	leads the procession

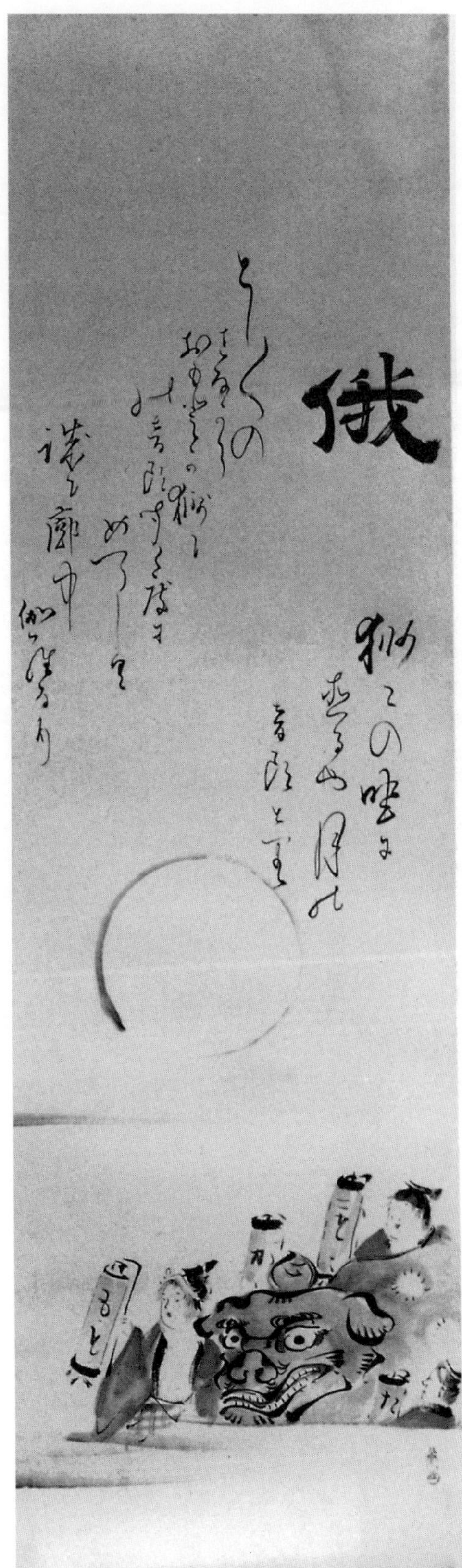
俄

44. Chōkōbō Roshōan (1797-1875)
Hotei

Ink on paper, 15 3/4 x 10 5/8 (40 x 27)
Private Collection

Roshōan, a haiku master from Mino, has here portrayed Hotei, one of Japan's most beloved subjects. A semihistorical wandering Chinese monk who preferred playing with children to living in a temple, Hotei became known as one of the "seven gods of good fortune" in Japan. He symbolizes happiness in the everyday world, which can be a form of Zen enlightenment.

Sometimes pictured with the other six gods of good fortune, now Hotei is alone. Leaning on his bag with his fan and staff behind him, he is gazing at the moon.

Rokunin no	Separated from
tomo o hanarete	his six friends —
yū suzumi	evening cool

Roshōan has elegantly constructed this image so that the circle of the moon suggests the curving shapes of the round head of Hotei and his bag. In contrast, both painting and calligraphy are constructed in a diagonal that supports the gaze of Hotei towards the moon. He seems pensive, perhaps even sad. Is he lonely, separated not only from his friends, but also from the moon by the calligraphy? Is this a visualization of how words can sometimes get in the way of direct perceptions? Or is he just an old monk, raising his face to the night sky?

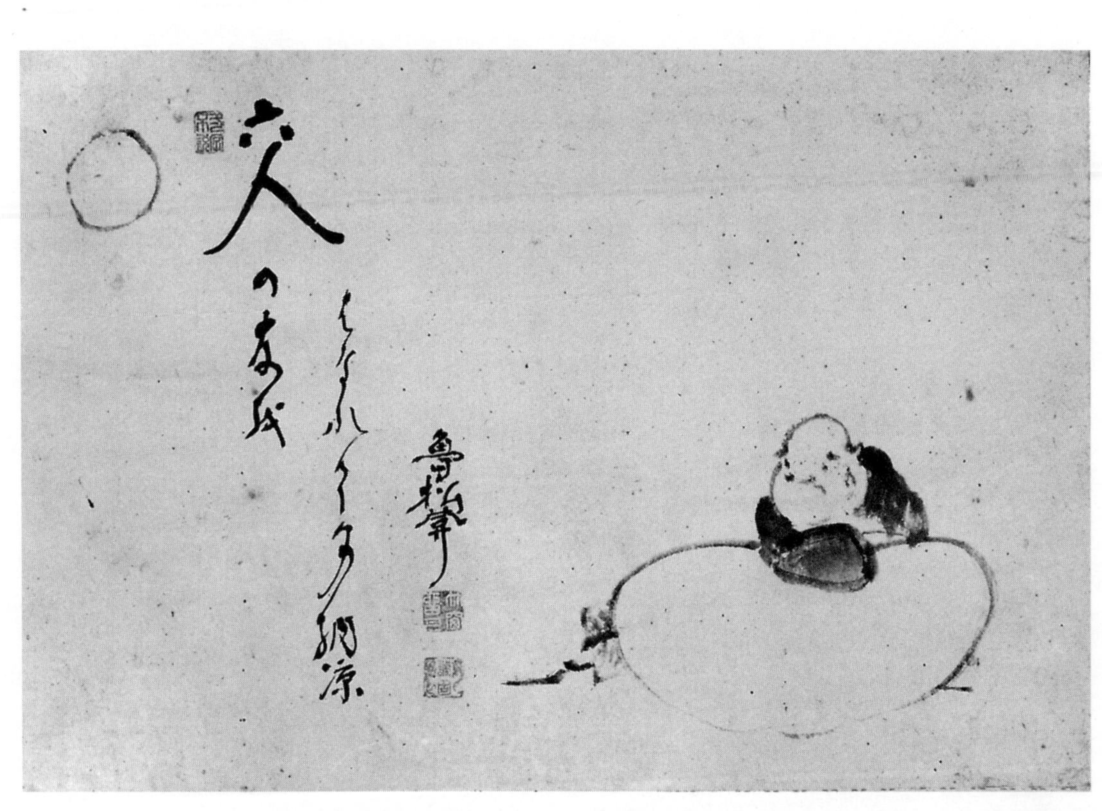

45. Hakuin Ekaku (1685-1768)

Bag of Hotei

Ink on paper, 16 1/2 x 20 1/8 (42 x 51.2)

Private Collection

Hakuin was the most important Zen Master of the past five hundred years in Japan. Living during an age when the government no longer supported Zen and society was becoming more materialistic, he revived the Rinzai sect Zen tradition, organized a series of *kōan* (meditation questions), and trained a number of disciples who carried on and spread his Zen teachings. Rinzai Zen to this day follows the Hakuin line of transmission.

As well as training his followers, giving public Zen lectures, and writing Zen texts and commentaries, Hakuin reached out to the public with paintings and calligraphy, often based on folk or popular subjects. He even utilized haiku, as well as Chinese-style and classical Japanese poetry, with his paintings. Here Hakuin has symbolized Hotei, the happy-go-lucky god of good fortune, by his attributes of bag, fan, and staff.

Neta uchi wa	While sleeping,
kami ka hotoke ka	a Shinto god? a Buddha?
nonobukuro	— just a cloth bag

Humor, not often encountered in religion, is a special feature of Zen, and Hakuin's haiku is full of puns. The first line of the poem can mean "while sleeping," but it can also signify "a leaning round fan." Therefore the main image can be seen not only as Hotei's bag, but also as a round fan put down to rest at an angle. Furthermore, as the scholar Joshua Mostow has pointed out, "Mr. Nono" (*nono-sama)* is Japanese baby-talk for gods and Buddhas. Hotei's name itself can mean "cloth bag." But where is Hotei himself?

Behind the series of meanings in the haiku is the understanding that even Hotei, whom we may consider a god or a Buddha, is really just an ordinary human who has discovered his inner Buddha-nature. In comparison with the Hotei painted by Roshōan (see Cat. No. 44), this image by a Zen Master is much bolder, and goes one step further than eliminating Hotei's six friends by eliminating Hotei as well. Hakuin confronts us with a close-up view of a paradox, and therefore, while this work qualifies as a haiga, it is even more a Zen painting.

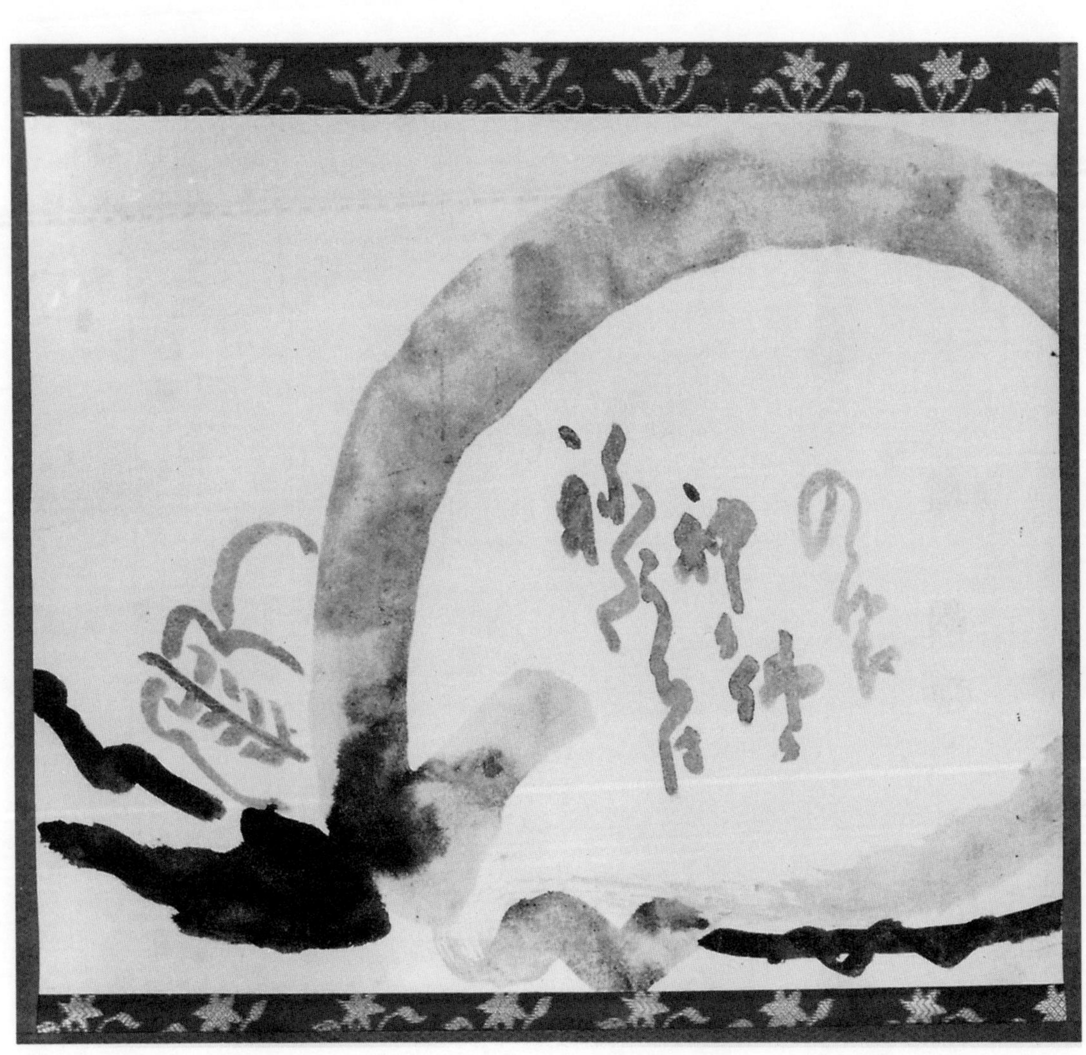

46. Sengai Gibon (1750-1837)

Three Gods of Good Fortune

Ink on paper, 40 x 10 1/8 (101.4 x 25.5)
New Orleans Museum of Art, Gift of Dr. and Mrs. Kurt Gitter

Sengai, a Zen Master from Kyushu, followed Hakuin's lead in creating painting and calligraphy to reach out to a wide public. He also had a marvelous sense of humor that shines clearly through his poetry and painting. Here he has depicted, in soft varied inktones, three of the popular "seven gods of good fortune." In front, Jurōjin represents long life with his extended forehead. Behind him is Ebisu, the god of angling, with his pole and a fish, and in the rear is Daikoku, the god of good harvest, standing on barrels of rice.

Sanpuku o	Three good fortunes
ippuku ni shite	transformed into one
taifuku cha	big fortunate tea

Although the three traditional figures represent long life, success, and wealth, Sengai suggests that human happiness can be much simpler. In Zen, the full understanding of our everyday life is enlightenment, while hungering after material goals is only illusion. Therefore, the greatest good fortune is to experience fully every instant in our lives, and enjoy a cup of tea.

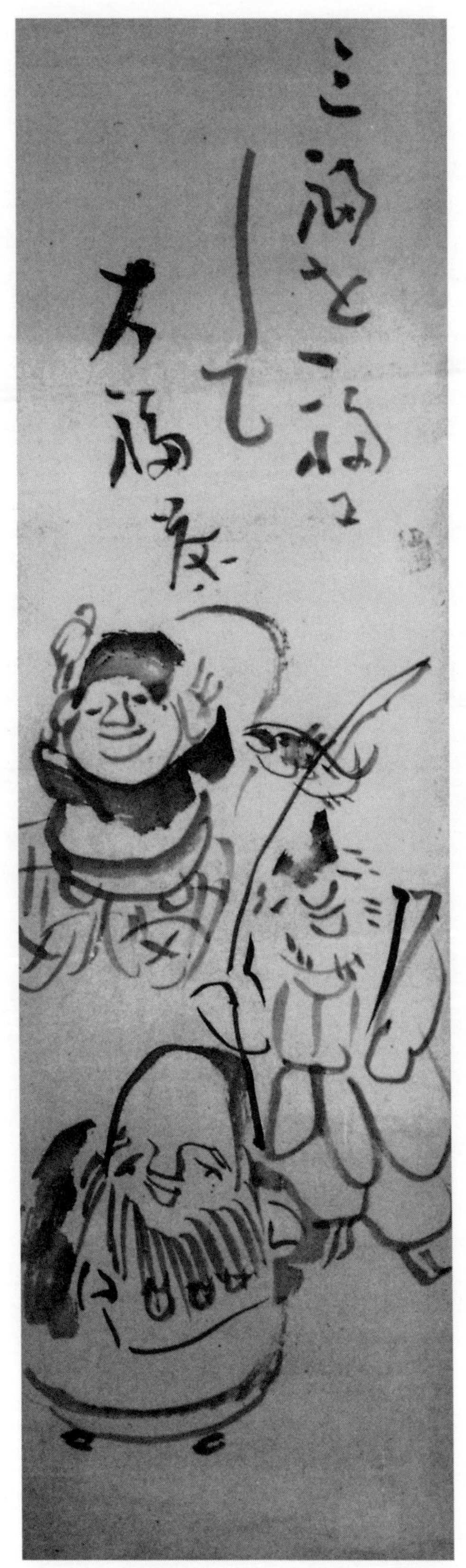
三福を二福に
して
大福哉

47. Nakahara Nantembō, also known as Tōjū Zenchū (1839-1925)
Ensō, 1924

Ink on paper, 51 1/2 x 12 3/8 (130.9 x 31.5)
Private Collection

Nantembō was an extremely dynamic monk-artist who helped to invigorate Zen teachings and Zen art in the first quarter of the twentieth century. He had a stormy career as an abbot, because of his lack of tact, but he was able to reach a great number of people with his lectures, *zazen* meditation sessions, books, letters, paintings, and calligraphy. Like Hakuin and Sengai before him, he turned to brushwork primarily in his later years as a direct expression of his Zen spirit, and several of his works are haiga.

Kono tsuki ga	If you want
hoshikuba yarō	this moon, I'll give it to you —
totte miyo	try to catch it!

The Zen circle called ensō is the most classic Zen subject since it can symbolize the universe, the void, the Buddha-nature, or only a rice-cake. Here one of its meanings is the moon, representing all that people search for outside themselves. Earlier Zen Masters such as Hakuin had pictured a monkey reaching for the reflection of the moon in the water, a symbol of impossible hopes and earthly illusions. But Nantembō is more direct, inviting us to catch the moon if we truly desire it.

Marcel Duchamp once said that every time we try and fail, we may have succeeded in something we did not know we were trying.

So what can we really catch here?

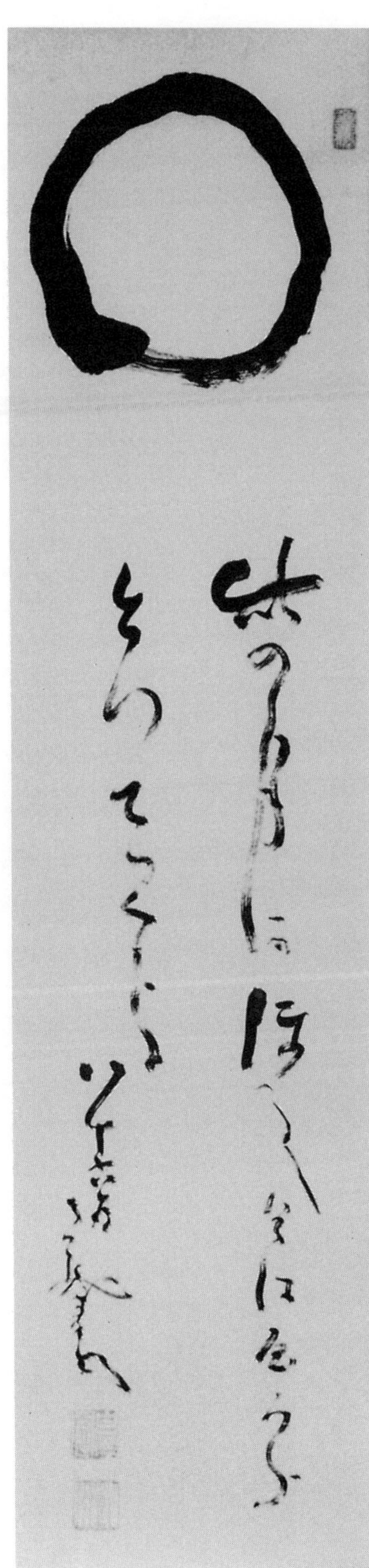

48. Kawabata Gyokushō (1842-1913)

Nihonbashi

Ink on paper, 44 1/2 x 12 1/2 (113 x 31.3)

Marsh Art Gallery, University of Richmond; Anonymous gift in honor of Charles Johnson

Gyokushō was one of the leading painters who spanned the transition from traditional painting to *Nihonga,* the new form of art that grew and flourished in the twentieth century. The word *Nihonga* literally means "Japanese painting," as opposed to oil painting and other techniques and styles from the West, and it features paper or silk, ink, water-based colors, and traditional brushes. Most *Nihonga,* however, has adopted a certain amount of Western perspective and shows less use of empty space than earlier Japanese art.

Gyokushō's first painting teacher was Nakajima Raishō (1796-1871), a master of the naturalistic Maruyama-Shijo tradition. Gyokushō then studied oil painting under the visiting English artist and cartoonist Charles Wirgman (1832-1891), but soon returned to his Japanese roots and became a professor at the Tokyo School of Fine Arts, teaching Maruyama-Shijō techniques.

In this haiga Gyokushō has reaffirmed his debt to Japanese tradition. He depicts only an outline of Mount Fuji and a small section of Nihonbashi, the famous bridge that opened the Tokaido Road from Tokyo towards Kyoto and Osaka. Everything else is suggested — the sense of adventure represented by the bridge, the power of Mount Fuji as a national symbol, and the unlimited possibilities inherent in empty space.

Gyokushō's haiku adds to, rather than describing, the image. He celebrates the tradition of family members joining together for a munificent multicourse meal on Japan's most joyous holiday:

Ganjitsu ya	New Year's Day —
mifūfu sorou	all three generations
zen no kazu	gathered for a feast

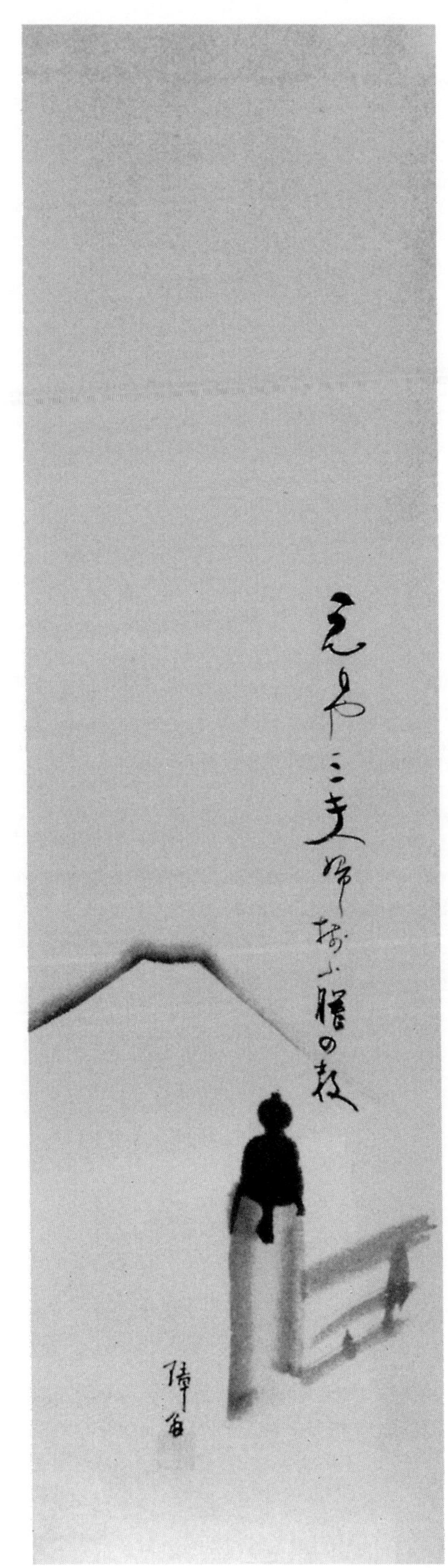

49. Hayashi Buntō (1882-1966)
Autumn Neighbors

Ink and color on silk, 13 x 11 1/2 (33.1 x 29.2)
Oliver and Yuki Behr Collection

The *kappa* is a unique Japanese creature who lives under bridges or near the ocean and causes great trouble and mischief for travelers. He gains his strength from contact with water, and since the top of his head is concave like a bowl, he always keeps some water there for strength. If you meet a *kappa,* the only way to escape trouble is to bow to him. He will bow back, the water will run out from the top of his head, and he will be powerless to do any damage. This myth demonstrates a typical Japanese response to uncertainty and potential danger: politeness.

Buntō's *kappa* wears a beach robe and covers his head with a kerchief as a disguise, but it does him no good, because the summer is over and everyone has gone. Whom can he fool now?

Hamagoya o	Shops by the beach
mina tozasarete	all closed and boarded up —
mushi no koe	insect voices

The calligraphy is distributed so that the first two lines of the poem are integrated into the willow tree behind the figure, while the final line, "insect voices," is all that lies ahead of the *kappa* as he stares into the distance. Buntō inscribed the lid of the box for this painting with his title: *Autumn Neighbors.*

After studying under the *Nihonga* artists Maekawa Bunrei (1837-1917) and Yamamoto Shunkyo (1871-1933), Buntō visited China several times. His style, however, is purely Japanese, with an emphasis upon humor and direct visual expression. The mournful expression of the *kappa* under the willow tree is doubly humorous, because he would surely be making trouble if there was anyone else around. But there are only the autumn insects.

[illegible]は[illegible]る
[illegible]戸さゝれて
[illegible]の[illegible]

文[illegible]

50. Iwaya Sazanami (1870-1933)

Samurai Hero

Ink and color on paper, 52 x 12 5/8 (132.2 x 32.2)
Oliver and Yuki Behr Collection

Like many writers and artists of his generation, Sazanami explored both Japanese and Western cultural worlds. Born the third son of the famous calligrapher Iwaya Ichiroku (1834-1905), he showed his scholastic talent as a youth, learning the German language thoroughly in order to read its literature. Sazanami's first publications came at the age of twenty, and he continued to be prolific throughout his life. He founded several magazines, beginning with *Young People's World* when he was twenty-three, and following it with *Young Women's World, Children's World,* and *Children's Pictorial.* As the leading Japanese writer for young people, Sazanami was especially interested in fairy tales, and he published collections of both Japanese and international stories for children while in his twenties.

At the age of thirty-one, Sazanami went to Berlin for two years, and then returned to Japan to continue his publishing and writing career. He became especially active as a haiku poet, joining noted poetry societies and publishing several books of his own verse. He also enjoyed painting haiga, often in a deliberately humorous style. Here he shows a samurai striding into the rain with his traditional oiled-paper umbrella; the poem can refer both to sword-fighting and the storm:

Hito furi ya	A single blow —
ide mono misen to	"here, I'll show you!"
yūdachi mo	evening shower

Sazanami's painting shows a dynamism rare in haiga. The samurai and his umbrella unite in a shape like the nosecone of a rocket, pointing up at a sharp diagonal. The force of the storm is equalled by the determination of the samurai, but in the Japan of the twentieth century, his only battle is with the wind and rain.

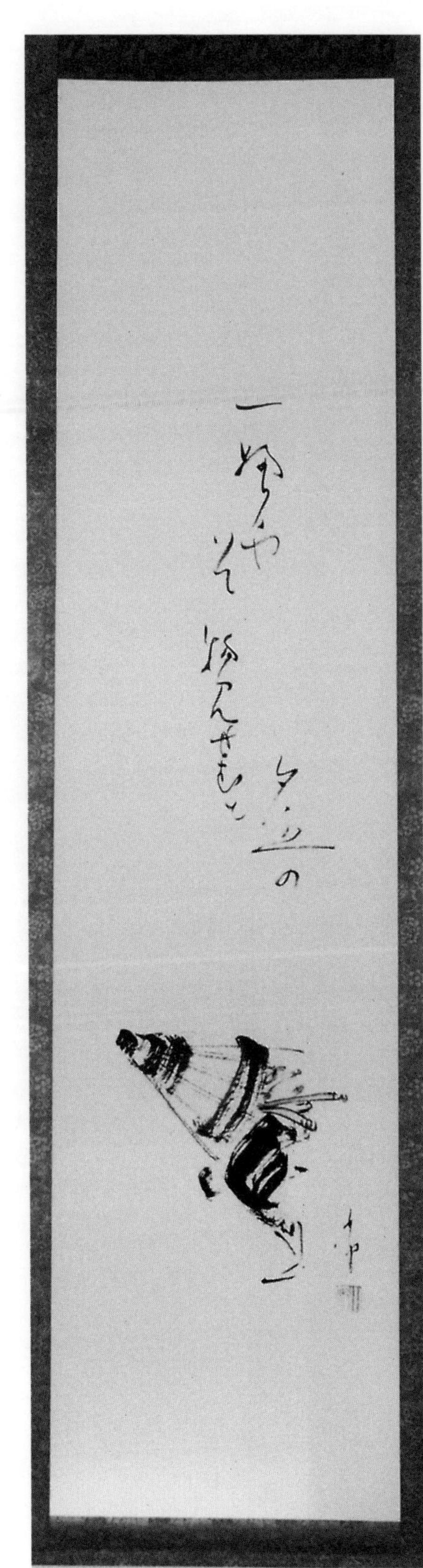

51. Hattori Kan'unshi (1883-?)
Poem by Taidō (dates unknown)
Snail, 1936
Ink on paper, 27 x 6 3/4 (68.8 x 17.2)
Private Collection

Kan'unshi (also known as Shun'yo) studied painting with the *Nihonga* masters Yamamoto Shunkyo (1871-1933) and Takeuchi Seiho (1864-1942), and then lived quietly in the Shōju-in subtemple at Daitoku-ji in Kyoto. This painting shows his great restraint; a snail crawls up the side of the scroll above the artist's cipher-signature. Nothing else — and yet the work conveys a great deal. The empty space offers viewers opportunities not only to enter the picture, but to experience the passage of time, as suggested by Taidō's haiku.

Aoba wakaba	Green leaves, young leaves —
roppyak- nen no	speaking of what took place
ōji kataru	six hundred years ago

This poem refers to a famous moment from Japanese semi-legendary history. In 1336, the nobleman Kusunoki Masashige fought for Emperor Go-Daigo against the Shogun's army. Realizing that his forces could not succeed, Masashige bade farewell to his son Masatsura at the post-town of Sakurai before his final battle and ritual suicide. Although the authenticity of this scene has been doubted by some historians, the parting of the nobleman from his son captured the Japanese imagination.

Because this moment is famous in Japanese consciousness, the word *aoba* (young leaves) has become associated with the young son soon to become an orphan. Further, the word *oji* means "past events," but with other characters it could also mean "Imperial" and "highway," giving the poem further resonance. The box inscription for this scroll says that it was painted and inscribed on May 17, 1936, during a period when veneration for the Japanese Imperial system was very high. Therefore we can understand that the cause of Emperor Go-Daigo, as represented by Masashige, was still important on its anniversary six hundred years later.

Perhaps the most imaginative feature of the haiga is the choice by Kan'unshi to paint a snail crawling up the side of the scroll. What might it represent? Could it be the slow passage of time? The persistence of memory that does not fade over six hundred years? The renewal of nature? Interpretations must be up to each individual viewer; this is one of the joys of haiga.

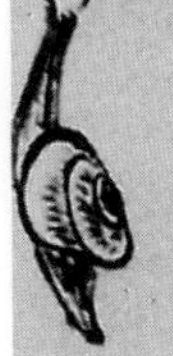

52. Shimomura Izan (1865-1949)

Old Man

Ink on paper, 14 1/8 x 3 (36 x 7.3)
Beckett Collection

Izan was born in Matsuyama on the island of Shikoku, but he lived most of his life in Tokyo. Talented in art as a child, his first success was as an oil painter in Western style. He had been born in the same village as the major haiku poet Masaoka Shiki (1867-1902), and together they formed an artistic group in Tokyo with the Zen monk Guan, the novelist Natsume Sōseki, and the painters Furuta Kodōjin and Nakamura Fusetsu. Shiki had long debates with Izan and Fusetsu about the values of Japanese versus Western art. Over a period of time, Shiki was convinced that Western art had great merit, but in turn Izan became much more interested in haiku and haiga. In his middle and later years, Izan turned increasingly to his native art traditions, painting haiga in a bold and free style.

Kangetsu ya	Cold moon —
waraji kaketaru	hanging up my straw sandals —
fuyu kodachi	winter trees

This small and simple work is one of Izan's most trenchant paintings, with a lone figure leaning against the cold (and also against the artist's cipher-signature). In Izan's few lines we can not only see, but also feel, the old man walking in the chilly evening. Why is this? Because of the roughness of line? The bending posture of the figure? His spindly shanks? Or more broadly, the lack of detail that allows us to use our own imagination?

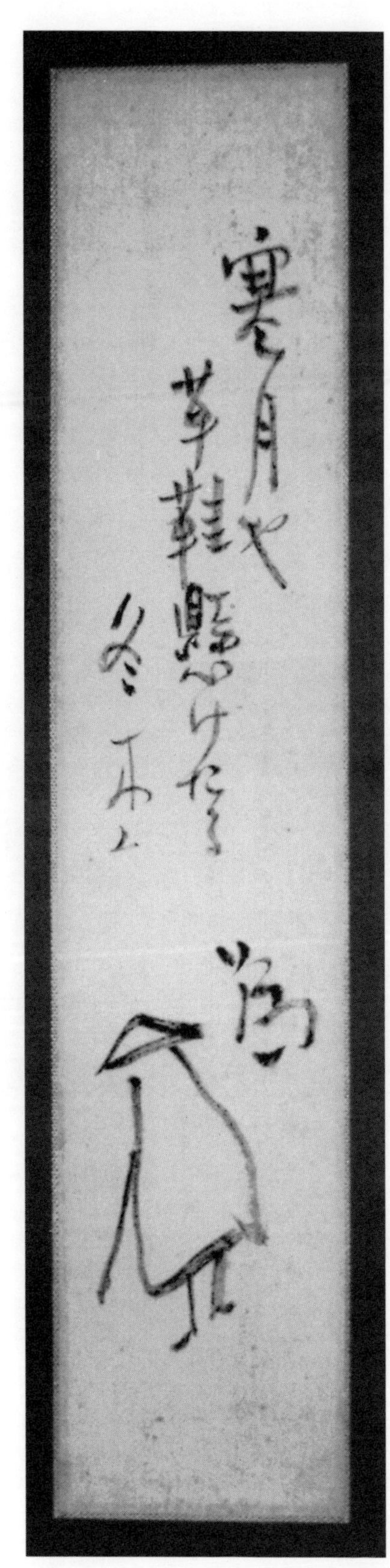

SELECTED BIBLIOGRAPHY

On Haiga in Western Languages

Calvin French et. al. *The Poet-Painters: Buson and His Followers.* Ann Arbor: The University of Michigan Museum of Art, 1974.
An exhibition catalogue of works, including haiga, by Buson, Goshun, Baitei, and Kinkoku.

Joan Hertzog O'Mara. *The Haiga Genre and the Art of Yosa Buson (1716-1784).* Ann Arbor: University Microfilms, 1989.
A doctoral dissertation examining Yosa Buson and his position within the history of haiga.

Peinture a l'encre du Japan (Nanga et Haiga). Geneva: Collections Baur, c. 1968.
A catalogue of paintings from the Heinz Brasch Collection of Zurich, including haiga by Yayū, Chora, Buson, Goshun, Sōchō, and Ayatari.

Schertsend Geschetst: Haiku-schilderigen. Belgium: Europalia, 1989.
The well-illustrated catalogue of an large-scale exhibition of haiga sent to Belgium from the Kakimori Bunko in Itami.

Leon M. Zolbrod. *Haiku Painting.* Tokyo: Kodansha International, 1982.
A large-format book written by a literature specialist that features large color photographs, with an emphasis upon Bashō, Buson, and Goshun.

On Haiga in Japanese

Bashō-ten (Bashō Exhibition). Tokyo: Keizai Shinbunsha, 1993.
The catalogue of an exhibition held at the Idemitsu Museum and the Kakimori Bunko commemorating the 300th anniversary of Bashō's death.

Bashō to Ōmi no monjin-tachi (Bashō and His Pupils from Ōmi). Otsu: Otsushi Rekishi Hakubutsukan, 1994).
The catalogue of an exhibition of seventy-one works.

Eiri haisho to sono gakatachi (Illustrated Haiku Books and Their Artists). Itami: Kakimori Bunko, 1992.
A catalogue of 186 early woodblock books on haiku with small reproductions of many illustrations.

Haiku (Taiyō Magazine, no. 16, Autumn 1976).
A special issue with short biographies of major haiku poets and many illustrations of their calligraphy and painting.

Inui, Norio. *Bashō-ō no shōzō hyaku-ei* (One Hundred Portraits of Bashō). Tokyo: Kōrinsha, 1984.
A catalogue of Bashō portraits by a great variety of artists.

Ishida, Motosue, ed. *Haijin shinseki zenshū* (Complete Collection of Genuine Calligraphy and Painting by Haiku Poets). Tokyo: Heibonsha, 1930-39.
A set of eleven volumes that average 200 black-and-white photographs in each volume. The quality of the reproductions is not high, but each work is given a reading in modern Japanese and there are short biographies of the artists.

Kakimori seishō (Prize Works from the Kakimori Bunko). Itami: Kakimori Bunko, various dates.
A series of catalogues of works of haiku and haiga, sometimes featuring specific artists such as Bashō (Vol. 2) or Buson and Goshun (Vol. 3).

Miyake, Chōsaku. *Haiga no kanshō* (The Appreciation of Haiga). Tokyo: Gahōsha, 1931.
An early discussion of haiga and its relationship with poetry.

Morikawa, Akira, ed. *Haijin no shoga bijutsu* (The

Calligraphy and Painting of Haiku Poets). Tokyo: Shūeisha, 1978-80.
A well-illustrated and thoroughly annotated set of twelve volumes on haiga that is now the standard in the field.

Ogata, Tsutomu, ed. *Bashō shinseki* (Genuine Paintings and Calligraphy by Bashō). Tokyo: Gakken, 1993.
A large and sumptuous publication with 150 color plates.

Okada, Rihei. *Bashō Buson.* Tokyo: Benseisha, 1976.
The catalogue of an exhibition held at the Itsuo Museum.

Okada, Rihei. *Haiga no bi: Buson Gekkei* (The Beauty of Haiga: Buson and Goshun). Kyoto: Hōshobō, 1973.
A book focusing on the haiga of Buson and Goshun (Gekkei).

Okada, Rihei. *Haiga no sekai* (The World of Haiga). Kyoto: Tankōsha, 1966.
A study of haiga by one of the major Japanese scholars in the field.

Okada, Rihei. *Me de miru haikai no rekishiten* (An Exhibition for Viewing the History of Haiku). Kōchi: Kenritsu Kyōdo Bunka Kaikan, 1976.
An exhibition catalogue of works from the Kakimori Bunko Collection.

Saikaku. Itami: Kakimori Bunko, 1992.
The catalogue of an exhibition of Saikaku's haiku and haiga.

Suzuki, Susumu. *Buson to haiga* (Buson and Haiga). Tokyo: Shōgakkan, 1976.
A study of Buson's haiga by a major scholar of Japanese literati painting

On Haiku in English (selected list)

Addiss, Stephen, with Fumiko and Akira Yamamoto. *A Haiku Menagerie.* New York: Weatherhill, 1992.
A selection of haiku about living creatures, in Japanese with English translations, illustrated with prints from old Japanese woodblock books.

Aitken, Robert. *A Zen Wave.* New York: Weatherhill, 1978.
A study of selected haiku that represent Bashō's deepening spiritual understanding, written by an American Zen Master.

Matsuo Bashō. *Narrow Road to the Interior.* Translated by Sam Hamill. Boston: Shambhala, 1991.
A recent translation of Bashō's most important haiku journey text, with haiga-style ink paintings by Stephen Addiss.

Blyth, R. H. . *Haiku.* 4 vols. Tokyo: Hokuseido Press, 1949-52.
A set of four books covering *Haiku in Eastern Culture, Spring, Summer-Autumn,* and *Autumn-Winter.* The poems, organized by season and theme, are given in Japanese with English translations, followed by short and pungent commentaries.

Blyth, R. H. *A History of Haiku.* 2 vols. Tokyo: Hokuseido Press, 1963-4.
Still the best history of haiku in English, including biographies of the poets in basic chronological order, a selection of their poems given in Japanese with English translations, personal opinions on their meanings and worth, and occasional black-and-white illustrations.

Henderson, Harold G. *An Introduction to Haiku.* Garden City, N.Y.: Doubleday & Company, 1958.
A general introduction to haiku and haiku poets, with word-for-word and rhyming translations.

Mackenzie, Lewis. *The Autumn Wind.* Tokyo: Kodansha International, 1984.
A biography of Issa and a selection of his haiku, given in Japanese and romaji with English translations.

Sato, Hiroaki. *One Hundred Frogs: From Renga to Haiku in English.* New York and Tokyo: Weatherhill, 1983.
An interesting study of renga and haiku,

including discussions of translation and composing haiku in English.

Ueda, Makoto. *Bashō and his Interpreters.* Stanford, Calif.: Stanford University Press, 1991.
A fascinating discussion of major Bashō poems, given in romaji, word-by-word translations, and poetic translations, followed by translations of historical Japanese commentaries (which often disagree with each other).

Yasuda, Kenneth. *The Japanese Haiku.* Rutland, Vermont, and Tokyo: Charles E. Tuttle, 1957.
An early study of the history and aesthetics of haiku, with comparisons to Western poetics. Some rhyming translations are included.

Yuki, Sawa, and Edith M. Shiffert. *Haiku Master Buson.* Union City, Calif.: Heian International, 1978.
Essays and translations of haiku by Buson, presented in Japanese, romaji, and English.

Basic Japanese Haiku Reference Works

Haiku shiriizu: Hito to sakuhin (Haiku Series: Poets and Their Works). 18 vols. Tokyo: Ōfusha, 1963-7.

Ichiji, Tetsuo, ed. *Haikai daijiten* (Large Dictionary of Haiku). Tokyo: Meiji Shoin, 1957.

Matsuo, Yasuaki, ed. *Haiku jiten: kinsei* (Dictionary of Early Modern Haiku). rev. ed., Tokyo: Ofusha, 1982.

Takagi, Sōgo. *Haikai jinmei jiten* (Dictionary of Haiku Poets). Tokyo: Meiji Shoin, 1960.